1 MONTH OF
FREE
READING

at

www.ForgottenBooks.com

By purchasing this book you are eligible for one month membership to ForgottenBooks.com, giving you unlimited access to our entire collection of over 1,000,000 titles via our web site and mobile apps.

To claim your free month visit:
www.forgottenbooks.com/free910627

ISBN 978-0-266-92467-8
PIBN 10910627

This book is a reproduction of an important historical work. Forgotten Books uses
state-of-the-art technology to digitally reconstruct the work, preserving the original format
whilst repairing imperfections present in the aged copy. In rare cases, an imperfection in
the original, such as a blemish or missing page, may be replicated in our edition. We do,
however, repair the vast majority of imperfections successfully; any imperfections that
remain are intentionally left to preserve the state of such historical works.

1910

MANUAL

FOR

COUNTY INSTITUTES

TERRITORY OF NEW MEXICO

COMPILED BY

C. M. LIGHT, T. W. CONWAY, J. E. CLARK

PUBLISHED BY THE
TERRITORIAL BOARD OF EDUCATION
SANTA FE, N. M.

1910
THE OPTIC PUBLISHING COMPANY
EAST LAS VEGAS, N. M.

TABLE OF CONTENTS

New Mexico Educational Directory

J. E. Clark, Superintendent of Public Instruction.
Acasio Gallegos, Assistant.

TERRITORIAL BOARD OF EDUCATION.

Meetings—Second Friday in September, December, March and June.

Gov. William J. Mills, President ....Santa Fe
J. E. Clark, Supt. Public Instruction, Secretary....Santa Fe
E. McQueen Gray ....Albuquerque
C. M. Light ....Silver City
Francis Marnane .... Santa Fe
W. E. Garrison .... Agricultural College
T. W. Conway .... Raton
W. G. Haydon ....E. Las Vegas
Blas Sanchez .... Wagon Mound

HEADS OF TERRITORIAL INSTITUTIONS.

E. McQueen Gray, President University of New Mexico
.... Allbuquerque
W. E. Garrison, President Agricultural College ....
.... Agricultural College
B. S. Gowen, President New Mexico Normal University .... East Las Vegas
C. M. Light, President New Mexico Normal School....
.... Silver City
E. A. Drake, President New Mexico School of Mines..
.... Socorro
Maj. J. W. Wilson, Superintendent New Mexico Military Institute .... Roswell
Mrs. George Dixon, Vice Principal Spanish-American Normal .... El Rito

W. C. Connor, Jr., Superintendent School for Deaf and
     Dumb .... Santa Fe
R. R. Pratt, Superintendent New Mexico Institute for
     the Blind .... Alamogordo
William Kirkpatrick, Superintendent Reform School
     .... Springer
E. L. Hewitt, Director of School of Archaeology..Santa Fe

SUPERINTENDENTS OF CITY SCHOOLS.

Albuquerque .... W. D. Sterling
East Las Vegas .... Rufus Mead
Clovis .... W. A. Poore
Raton .... T. W. Conway
Roswell .... M. H. Brasher
Santa Fe .... J. A. Wood
Tucumcari .... G. A. Danforth

PRINCIPALS OF INCORPORATED TOWNS.

Artesia .... W. L. Bishop
Alamogordo .... Chas. D. George.
Aztec .... W. G. Russell
Carlsbad .... V. L. Griffin
Clayton .... J. C. Campbell
Deming .... J. F. Doderer
Farmington .... L. M. Garrett
Gallup .... R. W. Twining
Hagerman .... D. A. Paddock
Las Cruces .... J. H. Wagner
Las Vegas .... Anna J. Rieve
Silver City .... W. B. McFarland
Socorro .... C. L. Davis

PRINCIPALS OF UNINCORPORATED TOWNS.

Amistad .... Ida Melton
Belen .... Mrs. Nora Brumback
Capitan .... Mrs. G. W. Smithson
Cerrillos .... C. L. Miller
Chama .... H. Ross Wood
Cimarron .... Cornelia Burke
Carrizozo .... E. B. Chapman

Central .... Clarence Link
Dawson .... C. E. Grover
Dayton .... H. G. Howard
Dexter .... S. L. Herriott
Elida .... A. E. Raidle
Espanola .... Ola Gilbert
Estancia .... T. N. Russell
Folsom .... Geo. L. Fenlon
Gibson .... Martha E. Savage
Heaton .... W. M. Marvin
Hillsboro .... J. E. Williams
Kelly .... P. A Marcellino
Kenna .... W. F. Irwin
Kirtland .... A. B. Bailey
Lakewood .... B. F. Kaiser
Lake Arthur .... Carrie Childress
Lincoln .... O. T. Nye
Logan .... R. E. Galloway
Lordsburg .... H. B. Copeland
Magdalena .... Joseph Daley
Manzano .... Reta Matthews
Melrose .... P. A. Grove
Montoya .... T. M. Spriggs
Mountainair .... Margaret Trimble
Nara Visa .... Willliam Buffman
Old Albuquerque .... Belva McCreedy
Portales .... Ben Smith
Pinos Altos .... Mrs. Griswold-Adams-Bisby
Roy .... , O. H. Kerns
San Marcial .... Mrs. M. S. Kelly
Santa Rita .... Ella Smith
Santa Rosa .... Frank Morris
Springer .... R. C. Bonney
Tierra Amarilla .... Laura Whitlock
Taiban .... Cora Freeman
Texico .... H. M. Pile
Torreon .... Lola B. Geisler
Tularosa .... R. S. Tipton
Willard .... J. I. Ferguson
Wagon Mound .... James Ellison

COUNTY SCHOOL SUPERINTENDENTS.

Bernalillo ....A. B. Stroup, Albuquerque
Chaves ....C. C. Hill, Roswell
Colfax ....Mrs. Josie Lockard, Raton
Curry .... L. C. Merstelder, Clovis
Eddy .... A. A. Kaiser. Carlsbad
Dona Ana ....Vincent May, Las Cruces
Grant ....Colin P. Neblett, Silver City
Guadalupe .... George Burch, Santa Rosa
Lincoln .... John A. Haley, Carrizozo
Luna .... Ney B. Gorman, Deming
Mora .... Blas Sanchez, Wagon Mound
McKinley .... M. Picard, Gallup
Otero ....L. Simms, Alamogordo
Quay .... C. S. Cramer, Tucumcari
Rio Arriba .... J. M. Chavez, Abiquiu
Roosevelt .... Mrs. S. F. Culberson, Portales
Sandoval .... Bonifacio Montoya, Bernalillo
San Juan .... M. F. Fifield, Aztec
San Miguel ....M. F. Desmarais, Las Vegas
Santa Fe ....John V. Conway, Santa Fe
Sierra .... J. P. Parker, Hillsboro
Socorro ....J. A. Torres, Socorro
Taos ....Isaac W. Dwire, Taos
Torrance ....Charles Burt, Mountainair
Union .... Joseph Gill, Clayton
Valencia .... Jesus C. Sanchez, Tome

SONG—NEW MEXICO

(Arranged from Byer's Song "Iowa" and dedicated to James
Elton Clark, upon his assuming the duties of Territorial
Superintendent, March 1, 1907.)

Tune: Maryland, My Maryland.

You ask what land I love the best,
New Mexico, New Mexico.
The fairest land of all the west,
New Mexico, New Mexico.
See yonder Rio Grande's stream,
Whose rolling waters brightly gleam,
O, fair it is as poet's dream,
New Mexico, New Mexico.

Alfalfa fields and tasseled corn,
New Mexico, New Mexico.
Where plenty fills her golden horn,
New Mexico, New Mexico.
See how her wondrous mountains shine
To yonder sunset's purple line,
O happy land, O land of mine,
New Mexico, New Mexico.

We read the story of thy past,
New Mexico, New Mexico.
What wondrous deeds, what fame thou hast,
New Mexico, New Mexico.
So long as time's great cycle runs,
Or nations weep their fallen ones,
Thou'll not forget they patriot sons,
New Mexico, New Mexico.
—Mrs. Geo. Dixon, El Rito, New Mexico.

TO THE INSTITUTE WORKERS

Probably no institute manual was ever prepared which thoroughly pleased all conductors, instructors and attendants upon the County Institutes. We have no genuine hope that this manual will prove to be an exception in this regard to those that have gone before. Our pamphlet for 1908 brought more general, enthusiastic and favorable comments than any other previously published by the Territorial Board of Education, but there are some leading institute workers who have called for outlines containing more of the professional phase of the various subjects, more emphasis upon method in the courses prepared for the first and second grade applicants, and it is in response to this suggestion that the Manual for 1909 was issued. So well did the latter seem to fulfill its mission that the committee decided to make very few changes in the manual for the present year.

It will be noted that the outlines in Part I are prepared for first and second grade applicants who attend the regular two weeks' institute. In Part III are outlines which may be added to those in Part I and combined for daily assignment when conditions warrant doing so. In some institutes the teachers are so well prepared and so interested in the work that the instructors find it very profitable to assign for discussion many topics not found in the regular outlines.

Part II is prepared for third grade applicants, and especially those who attend the four weeks' institute, in which there are to be twenty-two days of actual class work. Twenty lessons are prepared, but with frequent reviews and at least two written lesson periods which we would strongly recommend, we are quite sure that the outlines will present sufficient material. In the two weeks' institutes, the third grade applicants are expected to take the courses in Part II, but, of course, the work cannot be so thoroughly done.

Part III, as stated in the foregoing, may, in a measure, be presented in connection with Part I, but the instructors will find much material in these outlines which may very properly and profitably be presented during the General Exercise Period.

We would emphasize the fact that the courses in the Manual are to be followed closely. Some institute workers are inclined to TALK TOO MUCH. They fail to realize that the institute is a model school, and that the best instructor is the one who uses only a few words in getting the class members to make full recitations. Careful preparation should be made daily by the instructor or conductor, clear lesson assignments should be made, every member of the class should be required to present his work in good form, the art of questioning should be given close attention; in fact, the daily class work should be such as is found in the critic departments of a normal school. The questions given in the examinations held at the close of the institute are to be based on the outlines of the Manual, and the instructor cannot afford to sacrifice any time from the daily program, all of which is to be given to the outlines presented.

Note the following:

Assign permanent seats.
Prepare a daily register.
Insist upon punctuality and regular attendance.
Make the opening and general exercises interesting.
Sing often.
Adhere to good form in class movements.
Study the framing of your questions.
Secure well formed answers.

Hold each class member responsible for each lesson assigned.

If you must put off some question until "tomorrow," be sure to bring it up.

Don't "lecture" except at some evening meeting or after hours

Give the full time of the daily program to the work of the outlines.

In all third grade classes, give special attention to subject matter, but emphasize method in reading (combination of word, sentence and phonetic.) Discourage the use of the the alphabet method.

At the close of the institute, organize the teachers and others into a County Educational Association, and set the date for the first meeting. See that a wise program committee is selected.

J E Clark, Supt

Territorial Superintendent of Public Instruction. Santa Fe, New Mexico, May 1st, 1910.

THE COUNTY INSTITUTE

(Legal Phase)

Section VI. School Laws, Session of 1907. (Amended by section 6, Chapter 121, Laws of 1909). Teachers' Institutes.

The County Superintendents of Public Schools shall hold, or cause to be held, annually, in their respective counties, for a term of not less than two weeks, a Teachers' Institute, for the instruction of teachers and those desiring to teach. The County Superintendent of Public Schools, with the advice and consent of the Territorial Superintendent of Public Instruction, shall determine the time and place of holding such institutes and shall select conductors and instructors for the same and provide for the compensation thereof. No person shall be selected or shall serve as conductor or instructor who does not hold a certificate from the Territorial Board of Education authorizing him or her to do so. It shall be compulsory upon all persons who expect to teach in any school district, independent district or incorporated town, city or village to attend at least two weeks of the county institute or to show a certificate of attendance upon some county institute or summer school approved by the Superintendent of Public Instruction, held within the year. Teachers who hold third grade certificates or permits to teach, and who have taught at least three months of school during the twelve months previous to the time of holding any County Institute, may, upon attendance upon a county institute for a full term of four weeks, receive the sum of fifteen ($15.00) dollars from the Treasurer of the Territory, upon the order of the Territorial Auditor, of the funds arising from the rental or sale of the common school lands of the territory, upon presenting to the Territorial Auditor a certificate from the County Superintendent, in which the institute is held, and signed by the institute conductor and the Territorial Superintendent of Public Instruction, certifying that said teacher has complied with the provisions of this act; provided, any person, or persons, who may fail to attend by reason of sickness or other good and sufficient excuse rendered to the County Superintendent, and approved by him and by the Superintendent of Public Instruction, may be excused from such attendance; provided, further, that the Territorial Board of Education is hereby empowered to excuse such persons from attending the county teachers' institute as in its judgment it deems eminently qualified to teach by reason of their professional scholarship and training; and that nothing herein contained shall make it compulsory for cities which engage a city superintendent of schools who gives at least half of his time to direct supervision to hold such institutes.

The Territorial Board of Education is hereby empowered to issue a course of study for the Teachers' Institute. Authority is hereby conferred upon the Territorial Superintendent of Public Instruction to authorize the County Superintendent in any county wherein the conditions are such as to make it expedient to do so, to hold joint county teachers' institutes at such place as may be most convenient to all parties concerned, and when such power is delegated to a County Superintendent, the expense of such institute shall be equitably divided by the County Superintendents, subject to approval by the Superintendent of Public Instruction, among the counties participating therein. For the purpose of meeting the expense of the County Teachers' Institutes, County Treasurers of Class "A" shall set apart annually from the general school fund of their respective counties not less than one hundred ($100.00) dollars; in counties of class "B" not less than seventy-five ($75.00) dollars for such purpose; and in counties of Classes "C", "D,," and "E", not less than fifty ($50.00) dollars for such purpose. Provided that in counties where an institute is held for a full term of four weeks the County Treasurer shall set aside at least fifty ($50.00) dollars more than that already provided for institute purposes. At each session of the teachers' institute, the County Superintendent, upon the advice and consent of the Superintendent of Public Instruction shall collect from each person in attendance a fee of not less than one ($1.00) dollar, nor more than three

($3.00) dollars. The money thus collected and set apart shall be known as the "County Teachers' Institute Fund," and the County Treasurer shall be its custodian, but he shall not receive any of it for his services in receiving it, or as custodian thereof. All disbursements of the teachers' institute fund shall be upon order of the County Superintendent, countersigned by the Superintendent of Public Instruction, and no order shall be drawn on said fund, except for services rendered and expenses actually incurred in connection with teachers' institutes, but the legitimate expenses incidental to conducting examinations ordered by the Territorial Board of Education shall be considered as expenses in connection with the teachers' institute. Provided that the Territorial Board of Education shall have the power to waive the holding of any County Normal institute where authorized summer schools are held and in counties adjacent thereto.

A LEGALLY QUALIFIED TEACHER.

Section VIII.—School Laws, Session of 1907.

A legally qualified teacher, to teach in any school district, or incorporated town, city, village, or independent district, shall be one who has been certificated as prescribed by this act, and who possesses a certificate of attendance upon some county teachers' institute or summer school, approved by the Superintendent of Public Instruction, held within twelve months, or has an approved excuse for non-attendance. Any County School Superintendent, member of a board of school directors, member of a board of education, county treasurer, or other person, who shall directly or indirectly cause the public school funds to be paid for teachers' services to any other person than a legally qualified teacher under the provisions of this act, shall be guilty of a misdemeanor, and upon conviction thereof shall be fined in the sum of not less than one hundred ($100.00) dollars, nor more than five hundred ($500.00) dollars for each and every offense, and may be removed from office in the manner provided by law.

CERTIFICATION OF TEACHERS.

A person may become legally qualified to teach as follows:

I. By securing a county first, second or third grade certi-cate in any one of the following ways:

    A. By examination before the county superintendent at the close of the summer institute or at other dates set by the Territorial Board of Education. Institutes are usually held in August for two weeks. The County Superintendent forwards all examination papers to the office of the Territorial Superintendent of Public Instruction for grading.

    B. By presenting to the Territorial Board of Education satisfactory credits from Territorial Educational Institutions in those branches prescribed for the county certificates.

    C. By securing endorsement by the Territorial Board of Education of unexpired certificates granted in certain states or territories. This applies to cer-tificates equivalent, at least, to our county first grade certificate. Certificates of first grade or better are endorsed from Nebraska, Kansas, Oklahoma, Wyoming, Minnesota, Michigan and Missouri. Applicants with certificates from states not in this list must stand examination or submit credits from schools attended.

    D. By completing specified courses in specified schools.

    E. By graduating from the full course at St. Michael's College.

II. By securing territorial certificate (three year, five year, or life) from the Territorial Board of Education in one of the following ways—

    A. By satisfactory examination before the Territorial Board of Education in subjects hereinafter named.

    B. By securing the endorsement by the Territorial Board of Education of certificates granted in certain states or territories. (See C under I).

    C. By presenting to the Territorial Board of Education satisfactory credits from approved educational institutions in the United States. Application blanks and blanks for transcript of credits will be sent upon request. Transcripts must be certified by authorized persons in schools attended.

III. By securing a permit to teach from the county superintendent or the Superintendent of Public Instruction. These are issued to meet emergencies only and expire on the date of the next regular examination of teachers.

N. B.—In addition to the provisions of I, II and III, it is necessary, in order that one draw public money for services as teacher, to present a certificate of attendance upon the annual institute or an approved summer school, or to present an accepted excuse for non-attendance. A health certificate must be presented also.

IV. By meeting the requirements specified by city boards of education. Each city is a law unto itself in the matter of certificating its teachers, but certificates issued by a city board are legal only in the city where issued. Teachers in high schools and teachers of special branches, such as art and music, obtain their certificates as other city teachers do.

COUNTY CERTIFICATES.

Candidates for third grade certificates shall be examined in the following branches: Reading, Penmanship, Orthography, Geography, English Grammar and Composition, Physiology and Arithemtic. Third grade certificates are recognized for one year in any county in the Territory, and are granted on lower percentages than are required for second grade certificates.

Candidates for second grade certificates shall be examined in the following branches: Reading, Penmanship, Orthography, English Grammar and Composition, Geography, Arithmetic, Physiology, United States History, and an Elementary Course in Teaching and School Management. An applicant, to be entitled to a second grade certificate, must obtain a general average as high as 75 per cent, with no grade in any one branch lower than 50 per cent.   Second grade certificates are recognized for two years in any county in the Territory. Standings of 90 per cent or more in subjects on an unexpired second grade certificate may be accepted in granting a first grade certificate.

The law fixes the maximum salary for holders of permits and third grade certificates at fifty dollars; for holders of second grade, seventy-five dollars.

Candidates for a first grade shall be examined in Reading, Orthography, English Grammar and Composition, Penmanship, Geography, United States History, Physiology, Civil Government, Arithmetic, the Elements of Pedagogy—comprising a knowledge of School Management and Theory and Practice of Teaching—Elementary applied Psychology, and one of the following branches: Elementary Algebra, Elementary Botany, Elementary Zoology, Elementary Physics, or Elementary Bookkeeping. To be entitled to said first grade certificate the applicant must receive "a general average as high as 90 per cent, with no grade in any one branch lower than 75 per cent." These certificates are recognized for three years throughout the Territory, and at the discretion of the County Superintendent and upon the approval of the Territorial Superintendent of Public Instruction may be renewed once, if presented before the date of expiration.

Candidates for the first and second grade certificates shall be examined upon the same sets of questions in so far as the subjects are the same.

County and state certificates of a standard equivalent to that prescribed for a certificate issued by this Board, not lower than a county first grade, may be endorsed by the Superintendent of Public Instruction as county first grade certificates, limited to one year.   Such one year certificates may be extended by the Territorial Board of Education upon receipt of satisfactory evidence of one year's successful teaching.

TERRITORIAL CERTIFICATES.

In the administration of the law concerning the granting of territorial certificates the Territorial Board of Education makes its own rules. The following are the present rules:

Three grades of territorial certificates are granted, one for three years, one for five years, and one for life.

A territorial three year certificate may be granted to a candidate presenting any four credits (a credit shall consist of five forty-five minute recitations a week for a period of thirty-six weeks or its equivalent), named in Group II following, and all credits in Group I, except Observation (1-2), Practice (1)"; provided, however, that equivalents will be accepted for and credit in Group II, and for any credit in Group I, except "Psychology (1), History of Education, including a general knowledge of the following school systems—the German, the French, the United States, the New Mexico (1-2), School Management, Administration and School Economics (1-2), General Methods (1-2), Special Methods in Reading, Geography, Language, Spelling and Primary Arithmetic (1)."

After three years of successful experience the holder of a territorial three year certificate may be granted a territorial five-year certificate.

A person who has all the credits in Group I following and any four credits selected from Group II shall be considered as having the legal qualifications for a territorial five-year certificate; provided, however, that equivalents will be accepted for any credit in Group II, and for any credit in Group I, except "Psychology (1), History of Education, including a general knowledge of the following school systems—the German, thea French, the United States, the New Mexico (1-2), School Management (1-2), General Method (1-2), Special Methods in Reading, Geography, Language, Spelling and Primary Arithmetic (1)." Practice teaching shall be construed as consisting of actual teaching in elementary school under the supervision of a critic teacher. Five year certificates may be renewed for three years, if such certificates were not issued as extensions of three year certificates.

Twenty-seven school months of four weeks each of successful teaching will be accepted in lieu of the half-year of observation and the one year practice teaching specified in Group I.

On presentation of four credits in addition to those upon which the five year certificates are granted, approved by the Territorial Board of Education, a holder of a territorial five year certificate, after five years of successful experience, may be granted a territorial life certificate.

An applicant will not be granted a county certificate or a territorial certiifcate, except an honorary life certificate, unless his application is accompanied by a statement of the grades received in the branches prescribed, certified to by the proper authorities.

A fee of three dollars ($3.00) is charged for the three years' and the five years' certificates and ten dollars ($10.00) for the life certificate. Do not remit until after having received notice of favorable action upon your application.

GROUP I.

Arithmetic Review (with a view to teaching) (1), Geometry (1), Zoology (1-2), Algebra (1), English Grammar Review (with a view of teaching) (1), Composition and Rhetoric (1), History of English Literature and English and American Classics (2), United States History (1-2), Civics (1-2), General History (1), Physiology and Hygiene (1-2), Botany (1-2), Physical Geography (1-2), Psychology (1), History of Education, including a general knowledge of the following school systems—the German, the French, the United States, and the New Mexico (1-2), School Management (1-2), General Method (1-2), Special Method in Reading, Geography, Language, Spelling and Primary Arithmetic (1), Observation (1-2), Practice (1).

GROUP II.

Latin (2), (3), or (4), Spanish (2), Greek (2), German (2), Trigonometry (1-2), Sociology (1-2), Ethics (1-2), Geology (1-2), Astronomy (1-2), Commercial Law (1-2), English History (1-2), Chemistry (1), Bookkeeping (1-2), Physics (1), Calculus (1-2).

NEW MEXICO TEACHERS' READING CIRCLE ANNOUNCEMENT FOR 1909-10.

(For full information write to the secretary of the Reading Circle, Rupert F. Asplund, Santa Fe, N. M.)

The Reading Circle year began September first, 1909, and will close August thirty-first, 1910.

COURSES.

Books to be read during the year 1909-10:

1. *Civics and Health,* published by Ginn & Co., Chicago, Ill. Price, $1.25.

2. *Teaching a District School,* published by the American Book Co., Chicago, Ill. Price $1.00.

3. *The Recitation,* published by the J. B. Lippincott Company, Philadelphia, Pa. Price $1.10.

Civics and Health will be read by all the members.

Teaching a District School is intended for teachers holding permits, third grade certificates and for all who are working for second grade certificates.

The Recitation is for holders of territorial certificates and for those who have or are working for first grade certiifcates.

CREDIT.

At a meeting of the Territorial Board of Education, held March 24th and 25th, 1910, the following resolution was passed:

The Superintendent of Public Instruction is hereby authorized to base the outlines in Pedagogy, Elementray Teaching and School Management and Physiology and Hygiene as far as possible on the text books adopted for the Reading Circle work and to prepare county examinations on the basis of these outlines.

From and after July first, 1911, all applicants for renewal of county first grade certiifcates shall present certificate of having satisfactorily completed the work required by the Reading Circle Board as follows:

All such applicants on and after July first, 1911, shall present certificate covering the required Reading Circle Work for the year preceding.

All such applicants on and after July first, 1912, shall present certificate covering the required Reading Circle work for the two years preceding.

All such applicants on and after July first, 1913, shall present certificate covering the required Reading Circle work for the three years preceding.

From and after July first, 1911, no person who has previously held a third grade certificate in this territory shall be granted a license of this grade except upon presentation of a certificate showing that the applicant has satisfactorily completed the work of the Reading Circle Board specified for third grade certificate holders for the year preceding the date of application.

Applicants for third, second or first grade county certificates who have pursued the Reading Circle course as prescribed by the Reading Circle Board and receiving a grade of not less than 75 per cent on examination covering any one of the books prescribed shall be allowed for 1910 one per cent on their general average of examinations for each book for which credit is so given.

Examinations meant are the regular examinations held for county teachers' certificates.

Assignment of Adopted Texts, Basal and Supplementary, Showing Publishers and Prices Assigned to Grades or Years.

FIRST GRADE OR YEAR.

BASAL—

The Wide Awake Primer; Little, Brown & Co., Boston.
Brooks's First Reader; American Book Co., Chicago.
Medial Writing Book, No. 1; Ginn & Co., Chicago.
Van Amburgh's First Days in Number; Silver, Burdette & Co., Chicago.

SUPPLEMENTARY—

The Wheeler Primer; W. H. Wheeler & Co., Chicago.
The Art Literature Primer; Atkinson, Mentzer & Grover, Chicago.
The Art Literature, Book No. 1; Atkinson, Mentzer & Grover, Chicago.
The Jones, Readers, Book No. 1; Ginn & Co., Chicago.

SECOND GRADE OR YEAR.

BASAL—

Brooks's Second Reader; Am. Bk. Co., Chicago.
Medial Writing Book, No. 2; Ginn & Co., Chicago.
Reed's Primary Speller (in certain schools); Chas. E. Merrill Co., Chicago.
Walsh's New Primary Arithmetic (in certain schools); D. C. Heath & Co., Chicago.

Supplementary—

The Art Literature Book No. 2; Atkinson, Mentzer & Grover, Chicago.
The Jones' Readers, Book No. 2; Ginn & Co., Chicago.

THIRD GRADE OR YEAR.

Basal—

Brooks's Third Reader; Am. Bk. Co., Chicago.
Reed's Primary Speller; Chas. E. Merrill & Co., Chicago.
Medial Writng Book, No. 3; Ginn & Co., Chicago.
Language Through Nature, Literature and Art (in certain schools); Rand, McNally & Co., Chicago.
Walsh's New Primary Arithmetic; D. C. Heath & Co.. Chicago.
With Pencil and Pen; Ginn & Co., Chicago.

Supplementary—

The Art Literature, Book No. 3; Atkinson, Mentzer & Grover, Chicago.
The Jones' Readers, Book No. 3; Ginn & Co., Chicago.
Good Health, Gulick Hygiene Series; Ginn & Co., Chicago

FOURTH GRADE OR YEAR.

Basal—

Brooks's Fourth Reader; Am. Bk. Co., Chicago.
Reed's Primary Speller or Reed's Word Lessons; Chas. E. Merrill Company, Chicago.
Medial Writng, Book No. 4; Gnin & Co., Chicago.
Language Through Nature, Literature and Art; Rand, McNally & Co., Chicago.
Conn's Introductory Physiology and Hygiene; Silver, Burdett & Co., Chicago.
Walsh's New Primary Arithmetic; D. C. Heath & Co., Chicago.
Natural Introductory Geography; Am. Bk. Co., Chicago.
Webster's Primary (or Common School) Dictionary; Am. Bk. Co., Chicago.

Supplementary—

The Jones' Reader, Book No. 4; Ginn & Co., Chicago.
Town and City; Gulick Hygiene Series; Ginn & Co., Chicago.

FIFTH GRADE OR YEAR.

Basal—

Brooks's Fifth Reader; Am. Bk. Co., Chicago.
Reed's Word Lessons; C. E. M. & Co., Chicago.
Medial Writing Book, No. 5; Ginn & Co., Chicago.
Reed and Kellogg's Graded Lessons in English; C. E. M. & Co., Chicago.
Conn's Introductory Physiology and Hygiene; Silver, Burdette & Co., Chicago.
Walsh's New Grammar School Arithmetic, Part One; D.
Natural Introductory Geography; Am. Bk. C., Chicago.
C. Heath & Co., Chicago.
Webster's Primary (or Common School) Dictionary; Am. Bk. Co., Chicago.

Supplementary—

The Jones' Reader, Book No. 5; Ginn & Co., Chicago.
Town and City, Gulick Hygiene Series; Ginn & Co., Chicago.

SIXTH GRADE OR YEAR.

Basal—

Brooks's Sixth Reader; Am. Bk. Co., Chicago.
Reed's Word Lessons; C. E. M. & Co., Chicago.
Medial Writing Book, No. 6; Ginn & Co., Chicago.
Reed and Kellogg's Graded Lessons in English; C. E. M. & Co., Chicago.
Walsh's New Grammar School Arithmetic, Part One; D. C. Heath & Co., Chicago.
Natural School Geography; Am. Bk. Co., Chicago.
Webster's Common School (or Primary) Dictionary; Am. Bk. Co., Chicago.
Montgomery's Beginner's American History; Ginn & Co., Chicago.

Supplementary—

The Jones' Readers, Book No. 6; Ginn & Co., Chicago.
Control of Body and Mind, Gulick Hygiene Series; Ginn & Co., Chicago.

SEVENTH GRADE OR YEAR.

Basal—

Reed's Word Lessons; C. E. M. & Co., Chicago.

Medial Writing Book No. 7; Ginn & Co., Chicago.

Reed and Kellogg's Higher Lessons in English; C. E. M. & Co., Chicago.

Webster's Elementary Composition; Houghton, Mifflin & Co., Chicago.

Walsh's New Grammar School Arithmetic, Part Two; D. C. Heath & Co., Chicago.

Natural School Geography; Am. Bk. Co., Chicago.

Montgomery's Elementary American History (in certain schools); Ginn & Co., Chicago, or Leading Facts of American History.

Webster's Common School Dictionary; Am. Bk. Co., Chicago.

Supplementary—

The Jones Readers, Book No. 7; Ginn & Co., Chicago.

Control of Body and Mind, Gulick Series; Ginn & Co., Chicago.

EIGHTH GRADE OR YEAR.

Basal—

Reed's Word Lessons; C. E. M. & Co., Chicago.

Medial Writing Book, No. 8; Ginn & Co., Chicago.

Reed and Kellogg's Higher Lessons in English; C. E. M. & Co., Chicago.

Webster's Elementary Composition; Houghton, Mifflin & Co., Chicago.

Conn's Elementary Physiology and Hygiene; Silver, Burdette & Co., Chicago.

Montgomery's Leading Facts in American History; Ginn & Co., Chicago.

Boynton's School Civics; Ginn & Co., Chicago.

Webster's Common School Dictionary; Am. Bk. Co., Chicago.

Agricultural for Beginners, Burkett, Stevens and Hill; Ginn & Co., Chicago.

Supplementary—

The Jones' Readers, Book No. 8; Ginn & Co., Chicago.

To Patrons and Teachers:

The following is an official list of the text-books adopted at a meeting of the Territorial Board of Education, June 11th, 1907, for use in the first eight grades or years of all public schools of the Territory, during the period of four years beginning June 15th, 1907, and ending June 15th, 1911.

If the subjects represented by the books named in the Basal List are taught in any of the first eight grades or years of the public schools, the texts named in the list must be used. There can be no substitute for any of the books of this list. See penal clause, Sec. IX, Chapter XCII, Session Laws of 1907.

In some schools the children are able to read well more than the one reader assigned to the year's work. Some schools wish to use an additional drill book in arithmetic. The Territorial Board of Education has approved certain books for this purpose; see Supplementary List. All supplementary books must be approved by the Territorial Board of Education, and if any school wishes to use any book as supplementary which is not named in the following supplementary list, application should be made at once to the Territorial Board of Education by addressing the request to the Territorial Superintendent of Public Instruction.

BASAL LIST.

	Publisher's List Prices & Dealers' Retail Prices	Dealers Mailing Prices
Little, Brown & Company, Boston.		
The Wide Awake Primer	$ .30	$ .37
American Book Company, Chicago.		
Brooks's Reader, First Year	.25	.31
Brooks's Reader, Second Year	.35	.43
Brooks's Reader, Third Year	.40	.48
Brooks's Reader, Fourth Year	.40	.48
Brooks's Reader, Fifth Year	.40	.49
Brooks's Reader, Sixth Year	.40	.49
Charles E. Merrill Company, Chicago.		
Reed's Primary Speller	.20	.24

Reed's Word Lessons	.25	.30
Ginn & Company, Chicago.		
Medial Writing Books, eight numbers, per doz.	.65	.75
With Pencil and Pen	.35	.40
Rand, McNally & Company, Chicago.		
Language Through Nature, Literature and Art	.45	.55
Charles E. Merrill Company, Chicago.		
Reed and Kellogg's Graded Lessons in English	.40	.47
Reed and Kellogg's Higher Lessons in English	.63	.72
Houghton, Mifflin & Co., Chicago.		
Webster's Elementary Composition	.65	.75
Silver, Burdette & Co., New York.		
Conn's Elementary Physiology and Hygiene	.36	.44
Conn's Physiology and Hygiene	.60	.70
Ginn & Company, Chicago.		
Agriculture for Beginners	.75	.85
Silver, Burdette & Co., Chicago.		
Van Amburgh's First Days in Number ..		
D. C. Heath & Company, Chicago.		
Walsh's New Primary Arithmetic	.30	.37
Walsh's New Grammar School Arithmetic, Part One	.40	.47
Walsh's New Grammar School Arithmetic, Part Two	.45	.53
Walsh's New Grammar School Arithmetic, Complete Part 1 and Part 2, in one volume	.65	.77
American Book Company, Chicago.		
Natural Introductory Geography	.60	.75
Natural School Geography	1.25	1.50
Ginn & Company, Chicago.		
Montgomery's Beginners' American History	.70	.78
Montgomery's Elementary American History	.85	.95

Montgomery's Leading Facts in Ameri-
can History 1.15   1.33
Boynton's School Civics 1.10   1.22
   American Book Company, Chicago.
Webster's Primary Dictionary .... .48   .56
Webster's Common School Dictionary... .72   .82
Webster's High School Dictionary ..... .98   1.12
Webster's Academic Dictionary 1.50   1.70

SUPPLEMENTARY LIST.

	Publisher's List Prices & Dealers' Retail Prices	Dealers' Mailing Prices

(May be used in addition to, but not in
lieu of the texts in the Basal List.)
   W. H. Wheeler & Co., Chicago.
The Wheeler Primer ....$ .30 $ .37
   Atkinson, Mentzer & Grover Co.
The Art Literature Readers, A Primer.. .30   .37
The Art Literature Readers, Book One.. .30   .37
The Art Literature Readers, Book Two.. .40   .49
The Art Literature Readers, Book Three .50   ...
   Ginn & Company, Chicago.
The Jones' Readers (by grades), Book
One .... .30   .37
The Jones' Readers, Book Two ...... .35   .43
The Jones' Readers, Book Three ...... .45   .55
The Jones' Readers, Book Four ...... .45   .55
The Jones' Readers, Book Five .... .45   .55
The Jones' Readers, Book Six .... .45   .55
The Jones' Readers, Book Seven ...... .45   .55
The Jones' Readers, Book Eight ...... .50   .60
Wentworth and Hill's Exercises in Arith-
metic .... .65
   Thompson, Brown & Co., Boston.
Nichol's Arithmetical Problems ....
   Benj. H. Sanborn Company, Chicago.
Southworth's Exercises in Arithmetic.. .40
   G. & C. Merriam Co., Springfield, Mass.
Webster's International Dictionary ....

Ginn & Company, Chicago.

Good Health	.40	.45
Town and City	.50	...
Control of Body and Mind	.50	...
Emergencies		

Any person, patron, teacher, board of school directors, board of education, or dealer may order any quantity of the books in the foregoing list by addressing the publishers direct. At the prices given in the first column the publishers will prepay the postage or expressage on any quantity to any post-office or express office in the Territory, if cash accompanies the order; or if the person or dealer making the order is known by the publisher to be financially responsible, the money need not be sent with the order—orders may be made by telegraph in these cases.

The prices given in the first column are in practically all cases the regular retail prices of the books to persons who call at the dealer's place of business. In case any person wishes to order from a dealer and have the books delivered by mail, he should send with his order the price named in the second column. At the prices named in the first column the dealer cannot pay the transportation of any kind—postage, express or freight.

It is the intent of the law that there shall be a uniform series of school books used in all of the first eight grades of our public schools. The penalty for failing to comply with the law is very severe. Teachers, patrons and school officers are therefore urged to see that the law is carried out; for instance, every school must use the Brooks' Readers; every school must use the Walsh Arithmetic; every school must use Montgomery's Histories if history is taught in the school by the use of a text book; every school must use Reed's Spellers, etc. Jones' Readers may be used in addition to the Brooks' Readers, but they may not be used in lieu of the Brooks'.

Address inquiries concerning the question of text books to:

J. E. CLARK,

Territorial Superintendent of Public Instruction and Secretary of the Territorial Board of Education.
Santa Fe, N. M., May, 1910.

NSTITUTE DAILY PROGRAM

(Suggestive.)
ONE INSTRUCTOR.
Four Weeks Institute.

8:00— 8:15	General Exercises.
	School Management.
	Sanitation.
8:15— 9:00	Arithmetic.
9:00— 9:45	Grammar.
9:45—10:30	Geography.
10:30—10:45	Recess.
10:45—11:30	Study Period.
	Individual Help.
11:30—12:00	Spelling.
12:00— 1:15	Noon.
1:15— 2:00	Physiology.
2:00— 2:30	Penmanship.
2:30— 3:15	Reading.
	Special work in increasing vocabulary.
3:15— 4:00	Special help for next day.

N. B.—The four weeks' institute is in reality a summer school, and every possible help should be given the applicants. Conduct a model school. By example teach school management, lesson assignments, how to study, best recitation methods, etc.

INSTITUTE DAILY PROGRAM.

(Suggestive.)
ONE INSTRUCTOR.
Two Weeks' Institute.

NOTE—All teachers together in all classes. Third grade applicants should attend classes in History, Pedagogy, Psychology, etc., with first and second grade teachers.

Teachers are accustomed to the two session plan and will ordinarily do better work than when required to begin work at seven o'clock in the forenoon and continue till nearly one o'clock. For this reason the divided session plan is suggested. Of course, if teachers and conductor prefer the one session plan, they may adopt it.

Forenoon.

8:15— 8:30	General Exercises.
8:30— 9:00	Arithmetic.
9:00— 9:30	Grammar.
9:30—10:00	Geography.
10:00—10:15	Recess.
10:15—10:45	Reading.
10:45—11:15	Physiology.
11:15—11:45	History and Civics.

Afternoon.

1:15— 1:45	Pedagogy and School Management.
1:45— 2:15	Spelling and Penmanship.
2:15— 2:45	Psychology.
2:45— 3:15	Optional Subject.

INSTITUTE DAILY PROGRAM.

(Suggestive.)
Two Instructors.
Two Weeks' Institute.

NOTE—First and Second Grade applicants together. Third Grade applicants by themselves, but they should attend afternoon classes for obvious reasons.

	Instructor A	Instructor B.
8:00— 8:40	Arithmetic (1st & 2nd)	Arithmetic (3rd)
8:40— 9:20	Grammar (1st & 2nd)	Grammar (3rd)
9:20—10:00	Geography (1st & 2nd)	Geography (3rd)
10:00—10:15	Recess.	
10:15—10:55	Reading (1st & 2nd)	Reading (3rd)
10:55—11:25	Spelling & Penmanship (1st & 2nd)	
10:55—11:25		Spelling & Penmanship (3rd)
11:25—12:00	Physiology (1st & 2nd)	Physiology (3rd)

˙ Noon.

1:15— 1:30	General Exercises.	
1:30— 2:10	History.	
2:50— 3:30		Psychology
2:10— 2:50	Pedagogy	School Management
3:30— 4:10	Optional Subject.	
4:10— 4:30		Civics

N. B.—Of course, an exchange of subjects may be advisable in many cases on account of special preparation of one of the instructors in certain branches.

Rules for Conducting County Examinations.

1. Examinations shall be held on Friday and Saturday at the close of the County Institute, and at such other times as may be fixed by the Territorial Superintendent of Public Instruction.

2. Promptly at the time set in the program for the beginning of the examination in each subject, the County Superintendent shall announce the subject of examination and the time to be devoted to it. Thereupon he shall open the proper sealed packages of questions and distribute one list to each person to be examined.

3. Promptly at the close of the time allowed to the examination in any subject, the County Superintendent shall collect all papers and immediately seal them preparatory to mailing as directed by the Superintendent of Public Instruction.

4. During the examination the candidates shall be seated as far apart as possible and they shall not be allowed to communicate with each other; furthermore, there shall be no comment or explanation by anyone as to the meaning of the questions.

5. After having begun to write on a list of questions, the examinee must finish the list before intermission or before taking up another list.

6. At the head of each list the maximum of time to be allowed to each subject appears, and in no case shall additional time be allowed.

7. The County Superintendent shall furnish each examinee

at the opening of the examination with a copy of these rules, which must be followed implicitly.

(Adopted by the Territorial Board of Education, June 13th, 1907. See Section 3, Chapter 97, Laws of 1907.

EXAMINATION PROGRAM.

(Suggestive.)

NOTE—The following program of examinations is suggestive, merely. If you wish to make any changes, please write to the office of the territorial department of education, stating the nature of the changes desired. The time assigned to each subject is in accordance with the time allotted on the examination questions.

You will note that the third grade applicants will be able to complete their work on Friday; the second grade, by 10:30 Saturday, and first grade applicants will require the full two days.

When you have adopted your program, hold rigidly to it.

Observe the rules for conducting examinations, following the program.

Notify this office of all unfairness in examination. If any candidate uses helps of any kind or gets information by communication in any form, either dismiss him from the examination or report him for failure by making note on the papers as they are handed in.

EXAMINATION PROGRAM.

(Suggestive.)

Friday—

7:30— 9:00	Grammar. All grades.
9:00—10:15	Geography. All grades.
10:15—11:30	Physiology. All grades.
11:30—12:15	Orthography. All grades.
12:15— 1:30.	Noon.
1:30— 2:00	Penmanship. All grades.
2:00— 3:40	Arithmetic. All grades.
3:40— 4:40	Reading. All grades.

Saturday—

7:30— 9:00   U. S. History. First and Second Grades.
9:00—10:30   School Management and Pedagogy. First
            and Second Grades.
10:30—12:00 Civil Government. First Grade.
12:00— 1:30 Noon.
1:30— 3:00   Psychology. First grade.
3:00— 4:30. Optional Subject. First Grade.

Rules Concerning Examination Privileges.

1. The holder of an unexpired second grade certificate may build for a county first grade certificate by taking examination in subjects recorded on the county second grade certificate in which the standings are lower than 90 per cent. (School Management not considered.) These examinations need not all be taken at one time. The examinee is privileged to write a portion of the required subjects at any one of several examinations held during the life of the second grade certificate.

2. Applicants are allowed the privilege of writing at one examination on a portion of the subjects required for any license and on the remainder of those required subjects at any subsequent examination during the institute season, June to September.

3. Applicants who write for second grade certificates but fail to secure same because of low standing in certain subjects, may be allowed the privilege of rewriting in these subjects, provided they write on all subjects in which the standings are lower than seventy-five per cent.; and provided, further, that the rewriting takes place during the institute season, June to September.

4. Applicants for third grade certificates failing to secure such certificate because of low standings shall be required to rewrite on all subjects required for such license.

Instructions to Examinee.

1. Applicants writing for certificates should write name and postoffice address as well as name of subject and grade of certificate sought on the first page of each paper.

2. Writer's name and name of subject should appear on each separate sheet used to avoid possibility of loss.

3. Pages should be numbered consecutively. Questions may be answered in any order, but each answer should be numbered as the corresponding question.

4. If double sheets of paper are used it will be more convenient for the reader if such sheets are cut in two.

5. Write only on one side of the sheet. Use pencil or pen and ink.

6. Use paper of uniform size, preferably legal cap, or foolscap.

Instructions For Packing Papers.

1. Place papers written on each subject together, being careful to keep third grade papers separate from first and second grade subjects. Pack all papers flat.

2. Do not place any other papers in package with answers to examination questions.

3. Please forward all other papers of whatever kind to the office of the Superintendent of Public Instruction, Santa Fe, New Mexico.

Part I
ADVANCED COURSES
FOR
First and Second Grade Applicants

ARITHMETIC

Lesson I.

Nature and Number.

1. The clarified number concept involves at least three ideas: (1) A measured quantity, (2) a measuring unit of the same kind, and (3) the expressed relation of the two. Define number. Number arises in the mind by observation, comparison, and judgment. What has number to do with the qualities of objects? Illustrate. What are abstract numbers? Concrete numbers?

2. What is rational counting? Does the child have the conception, "the how many," when he repeats the numerical adjectives, even though he may apply them to the objects? What are the tests of rational counting? In case a child cannot count, what is his starting point? What expressions does he use to show the vague muchness of his ideas? At what point in the counting would you show that ten units make one ten? How far would you count by naming the successive numbers before grouping them?

3. What is meant by saying that number is a tool of measurement? What is a unit? An unmeasured unit? Give the standard units of measurement. What advantages do these standard units possess over the unmeasured units? What is a varying unit of measurement? What is the mathematical unit? Fractional unit? A decimal unit? The unit of percentage? When in the course of instruction should each of these units be introduced?

(At the end of these lessons may be found a list of problems taken from the adopted text, a certain number of which may be assigned for work each day.)

LESSON II.

Primary Methods—Two Ways of Presenting Numbers.

The history of primary number teaching shows the invention of many methods of presenting numbers to the learning mind. These naturally fall into two groups:

1. The old methods began with the mechanism of number The child first studied the language of number. He was taught to count and read figures without reference to objects. He next learned the combination of figures. Reproduce the tables of elementary combinations. Pupils were taught to write figures and then to read them. The mechanism of the fundamental process was learned in order: First, by learning the rules; second, by performing the process; third, by solving problems involving these mechanisms. These methods attempted to proceed from the abstract to the concrete, thus reversing the natural order of learning. Enter into a free discussion and criticism of these methods.

2. But the number concept can only arise in the mind by dealing with quantity. A recognition of this fact caused a more rational group of primary methods to appear. In all these methods three classes of exercises were provided: First, whether a single number was to be developed, or a combination of numbers taught, objects were employed to do it. Second, the combination was given numerical expression, the process being performed again and again by the symbols of number until fixed in the mind for future use. Third, the application in simple practical problems followed. Illustrate each of these steps in primary number work through addition, subtraction, multiplication and division. As a result, the old methods of primary number teaching were reformed to harmonize with these steps. While it has peculiarities of its own, the Grube method uses these steps of presentation. The Grube method teaches each number from one to one hundred through addition, multiplication, subtraction and division (notice the order) exhaustively.

Write out the Grube table for four and compare it with the table of fours of the old plan. What are your criticisms of the Grube method? What contributions has it made? What is the ratio method? Show how easy it is to get up a method of teaching number.

LESSON III.

Principles of Rational Number Teaching.

The best methods of teaching primary arithmetic, while holding fast to the real contributions of the past, are working along these lines:

1. The motive of learning number must come from the exercise itself. The child should learn number not for future. but for immediate use. He is put at constructive work which calls for a knowledge of number combinations. These combinations are then drilled upon and kept fresh by their applications as a means for the solution of new problems.. Thus the learner at every step in his course is made to feel a personal need for a knowledge of number.

2. Nevertheless the arrangement of the course of study proceeds according to the development of the number concept from a logical point of view. The teacher thinks out the successive steps or lesson units as he has done in the past and always must do. In all the newer methods these relations remain unchanged, but the methods of taking these steps, of presenting these lesson wholes, have become more rational.

3. Much of the material considered as essential in the old arithmetics has been omitted in the new. How would you determine the value of the material to be used? The answer to two questions will do this. Has the material itself a practical value? Is its knowledge necessary in order to obtain a knowledge of something else that is of practical value? State other values of arithmetic.

4. Our older books on arithmetic presented a topic exhaustively before passing on to the next. All the steps in addition were presented before taking up those in subtraction. Common fractions were finished before decimals were considered at all. We now present the subject in concentric sections for each topic considered. Explain the Spiral System as used by the adopted text.

5. The old method provided preparatory routine drills which became the tools for thinking out problems that followed. We now lead the child to think from the beginning. The data is given him and he works out his own problems. If he fails in this the teacher either goes back and leads up to the difficulty step by step or else puts it in a simpler form.

LESSON IV.

Language of Number.

1. Number has its own language forms. Upon first enter-- ing the school, how much does the child know of these? What is the difference between a figure and a number. When and how would you teach the Arabic figures? The Roman figures?

2. Four methods of expressing number and number rela- tions: (1) By figures, (2) By words, (3) By signs, (4) By position. Fully illustrate all these.

3. The long drawn out process of arithmetic requires three direct distinct language forms: (1) Definitions, (2) Explana- tions, (3) Rules. When should definitions be taught? By an ex- ercise in addition show the difference between the language forms of explanation and those of rules. Illustrate how the pupil should be taught these three forms inductively.

4. We set forth the meaning of problems, (1) by solutions and (2) by analysis. Show by the following problem the dif- ference, especially in the order, between its written solution and oral analysis. A block of stone is 12 inches long, 6 inches wide and 4 inches thick. Find its weight if 9 cubic inches weighs 2 pounds.

5 Compare the value of oral and written exercises. Does accuracy and rapidity in one form signify the same character- istics in the other?

The analysis may take three forms, (1) the silent, (2) the oral, (3) the written. Illustrate and discuss the value of these.

6. Discuss the value of long and short forms.

LESSON V.

The Child's Number Interest.

1. No extreme method should be adopted by any teacher, but the best of every method should be known as far as possi- ble. Illustrate this in the teaching of Percentage; Interest.

2. Should the content of the problem or the so-called appli- cation be taken from the child's or from his social relations?

3. How would you teach those problems, business transac-

tions, for instance, which the learner with his present expe-
1'ence is unable to picture to his mind?

4. How are good thinking and good language cor-ordi-
nated?

5. Discuss the question of interest—(1) challenging effort, (2) games and puzzles, (3) construction, (4) supplementary problems, (5) racing, (6) reviews, etc.

LESSON VI.

Elementary Combinations.

1. There are three processes that should precede these combinations: (1) Oral counting, (2) Reading numbers, (3)
Writing numbers. How are these dependent upon each other?'
In what order should they be taught? How are they related
to the elementary combinations?' What is group counting?
How much of these should be taught the first year? The
second year? How far would you carry place reading? When
you combine a digit with one, is it adding or counting?

2. Write all the possible pairs of the nine digits. Why
are some of them easier to learn than others? Would you
present the combinations in the order of the size of their
sums? There are two forms of expressing these combinations, the vertical and the horizontal, using the sign. When
should each of these be taught? When would you teach
column adding?

3. Is there any advantage to be gained in the so-called
Austrian method of subtraction by addition, over the especially learned subtraction?

4. Multiplication combinations may be presented (1) By
objects grouped and counted, (2) By using column addition.
Should these two methods be taught independently or should
they supplement each other? Is there any difficulty in teaching reverse multiplications. Why? What advantage is there
in counting by 2's, 3's, etc.?

5. Is there any need for a division table? Illustrate what
is meant by unequal division. When should this be introduced? Illustrate by the use of objects. Does the division
by *one* present any difficulty?

6. How would you deal with children that had any difficulty in learning the elementary combinations?

Fundamental Processes.

1. *Addition.*—(1) Adding pairs of digits—direct and reverse. (2) Column addition. (3) Two or more column addition, involving carrying. What pairs of numbers make the sums from two to eighteen? In two column or more addition, would you add each column separately and then the partial sums, or would you carry mentally and write the complete sum?

2. *Subtraction.*—(1) Austrian method by addition. (2) Subtraction that involves borrowing. (3) Zero difficulties. (4) Proofs by addition. Explain the process of borrowing by the use of objects. Give steps in unit and column subtraction. Illustrate the proper method of making change.

3. *Multiplication*—(1) One digit multiplied by another and reversed. (2) Product given and the numbers required. (3) Column multiplication involving partial products. Give the steps in graduation in passing from the elementary combination to the complete column multiplication. Would you teach these processes mechanically or would you teach them understandingly? How can you best dispose of the zero difficulties?

4. *Division.*—(1) Is it necessary to have a division table for special treatment? (2) Work out all the steps to a complete knowledge of the process of division. (3) In teaching long and short division, the one that presents the least number of difficulties should be taught first. Which is it? Show how unequal division will help in teaching these processes. Shall division by a one figure number be taught in its complete form before taking up two figures? (4) Explain division by measuring and partition. Does this distinction have anything to do with the skill in manipulation? (5.) Point out the zero difficulties. Is there any order of presenting these? (6) When would you teach proofs for multiplication and division?

5. Illustrate the well defined steps in each of the fundamental processes by the use of counters. (2) Set forth lucid explanation of each, using the terminology of units, tens, etc. (3) Write out a rule for each process and show how you would develop it. What are the advantages to the pupil in

teaching these? Which is more important, the explanation of these processes or that of the applied problems?

6. How much of these processes should be taught in the first four years or grades?

7. How many years should the child be in learning the elementary combinations of the nine digits?

Lesson VIII.

Measurement.

1. *Forms*—(1) Single things, (2) Value, (3) Extension, (4) Capacity, (5) Time, (6) Weight. Give the subordinate divisions of these measurements and repeat the table for each. What has given rise to each of these? Give their history. Give the fundamental unit of each table. Give the commercial use of each. What tables or denominations should be omitted in teaching? Why? Most of the units of each table should be taught objectively and separately. In your judgment what are they? Give your reasons. Trace the order of introducing these measures through the adopted text. Why is this order followed. Illustrate the forms of solution and explanation descending and ascending. Should these be taught exhaustively, table by table, or should the concentric method be followed? Why?

2. *These forms of measurement in relation.*—Explain how some of these tables have been derived from others. Explain also how this fact may be used in teaching them. If an article can be measured by two of them in a commercial transaction, which should be used? Show how objects that have been measured in terms of one table may also be known in terms of another through a common measuring unit. Give these units.

3. *Fundamental Processes.*—(1) Select from the text, solve, and explain one exercise involving addition, subtraction, multiplication and division, one each from all the tables. (2) Add 3-4 bu., 1-3 pk. Show the proper form of solution and explain the process as you would have your pupils do. (3) Subtract 1 rd., 3 yd., 1 1-2 ft., 2 in. from 8 rds., 2 1-2 yd., 2 ft., 1 in. and reduce to the simplest form.

4. Make out a grocery bill of ten items and receipt it, drawing your own form.

5.   Would you measure wood by cubic measure or by the cord foot? Explain the two methods.

6.   Show how to think and solve problems of areas. Problems involving cubic contents. Show how problems may be illustrated by diagrams drawn to a scale.

7.   Explain method of measuring lumber.

Lesson IX.

Fractions.

1.   *Nature.*—What is meant by friction? Define its terms. Show that both enumerator and denominator are measured quantities. Distinguish common from decimal fractions.

2.   *Reduction.*—What is the principle involved in reduction? Arrange the forms of reduction according to the order of presenting them in teaching. Select an exercise from each case, submit its solution, explain it and illustrate it by a diagram.

3.   *Fundamental Processes.*—Arrange a set of exercises under each of these according to their order of difficulty. Show a good form of solution for problems of each process. Would you teach the complex forms of fractions? Why? Explain why it is convenient to invert the divisor in division, in at least two ways.

4.   *Teaching.*—Why should the teaching of decimals follow after the common fractional forms? How early should the teaching of fractions be introduced? Group the fractional units according to the order of difficulty in presenting them.

5.   *Decimals.*—(1)   Explain how decimals may be written and read. (2)   Show that the decimal point presents no difficulty in addition and subtraction. (3)   Explain the pointing of decimal multiplication. In getting .05 of 362, first get one one-hundredth of the multiplicand and then the required product. (4)   Division that involves decimals.—Think or make the divisor and dividend of the same denomination, then observe that if the divisor is contained at all in the portion of the dividend of the same denomination, the quotient will be a whole number, otherwise a decimal. Explain.

(6.)   (1)   What does each of these problems mean?
            Divide 36 acres by 6.
            Divide 36 acres by 6 acres.

(2) Explain. If 3-4 of a ton of hay cost $8 3-5, what is the cost of 6 tons?

(3) What does multiplied by 3-4 mean?

(4) How do you explain the reduction of decimals to common fractions, and vice versa?

(5) Give rules for all operations in fractions and explain how you would develop them.

(6) Analyze: 7-8 is 3-5 greater than what number?

Lesson X

1. Show how you would teach the meaning of per cent (%).

2. Make a table of per cents written (1) with per cent signs, (2) as a decimal, (3) as a common fraction.

3. Make a list of problems showing steps of difficulty in the three cases of per cent. (1) Find 4 per cent of 25, (2) 10 is 25 per cent. of what? (3) 5 is what per cent of 15?

4. Solve the following problems by three methods, (1) hundred per cent, (2) the fractional, (3) the formula.

(1) A man owned a horse which cost him $90. He sold him so as to gain 33 1-3 per cent. What was his selling price?

(2) A note of $400 was credited with $150. What per cent. was paid? Remained unpaid?

(3 A man failing in business paid A $60, which was 16 2-3 per cent. of what he owed him. How much should A have received?

5. Explain how you would develop the following methods of interest: (1) Aliquot parts, (2) By years and fraction of a year, (3) By the 6 per cent. method.

Problems for Each Day.

First, explain these problems in a general way from the book. Second, solve them and place their solution on the blackboard. Third, explain these solutions before the institute. Give the best form of solution and explanation; especially let the English be correct.

Article 184, Nos. 15, 22, 35, 38, 45, 64, 92.

Article 230, Nos. 4, 7, 10, 12.

Article 248, Nos. 2, 11, 25, 38, 48, 53, 56, 62, 73, 83, 93, 94
Article 301, Nos. 9, 11, 20, 21, 41, 47, 50, 62, 83.
Article 312, Nos. 11, 16, 19.
Article 318, Nos. 4, 12, 13, 23.
Article 320, Nos. 31, 33.
Article 331, Nos. 2, 3.
Article 344, No. 5.
Article 347, Nos. 4, 5, 9, 10, 12.
Article 356, Nos. 1, 10, 11.
Article 375, Nos. 7, 12, 14, 19.
Article 380, Nos. 17, 20, 24.
Article 387, Nos. 8, 12, 19.
Article 390, Nos. 3, 11, 22, 37, 49, 71, 78, 95, 108, 117, 124
Article 405, No. 10.
Article 407' No. 11.
Article 428, Nos. 4, 5.
Article 461, Nos. 1 to 14.
Article 463, Nos. 8, 9.
Article 471, Nos. 6, 9, 13.
Article 515, Nos. 13, 35, 49, 64, 69, 87, 111, 123, 127, 129, 134.
Article 618, No. 9.
Article 631, Nos. 29, 32.
Article 634, No. 42.
Article 635, No. 52.
Article 638, Nos. 72, 101, 102.

Language and Grammar

LESSON I.

1. Define Language. Explain what is meant by saying that language is a movable type, that it is the support and vehicle of thought. Is there a faculty of language? Why does not the young child talk? What senses are concerned in the use of language? Compare the oral and written as to form, use and purpose.

2. Motives for using language.—(1) There is a force in the thought itself that urges to expression. (2) Language is a social affair. (3) We learn it largely by imitation and association. (4) The student must pride himself in the correct use of language—must have the language interest. (5) The child learns language under the impulse of a personal need. (6) The use of language is stimulated by having some immediate end in view.

3. Principles to be observed in the teaching of language: (1) The development of language and thought must proceed together. Knowledge is a growth and language should be. This applies to the manner and to the sequence as well as to the forms of language. If the pupil comes to the high school not able to write good English whose fault is it? The primary or the grammar school? The language work should be correlated with the other studies of the curriculum. This is not only economy, but this subject matter furnishes the strongest motive for expression. (3) The various language exercises are reducible to a few kinds; reproductions, conversations, descriptions, narrations, expositions, etc. To adapt these forms to the various grades requires the highest skill in teaching. (4) When models are made a separate object of study they should be put into immediate and constant use, thus becoming habitual mode s of expression. (5) Thus arises skill, freedom, rapidity and even versatility in composing. See that the child writes out of the fullness of

his personal experiences; learns thereby to talk with his
pencil as well as with his tongue. Discuss too much and
too little work. What is a labored composition? How
long should the composition be? Choice of topics. (6)
The teacher must supply an immediate end for talking and
writing. A pupil may be called upon to give supplementary information on a special topic from the history or geography lesson. The play instinct may be utilized in dramatization. A formal program calls for formal preparation and
special aid from the teacher. The pupils might be called upon
to face each other in debate or other formal contests. (7)
Talking and writing should complement each other. (8)
The study of forms, reading and composition should be separate exercises. They are along separate lines and exclude one
another. Would you correct pupils while composing or reading? (9) Every lesson should be a lesson in good English,
the teacher guiding so as not to interfere with the smoothness
of expression. Do not be too exacting. (10) Speech lags
behind the thought—"Ideas before words," therefore the
language work should be a little in advance of the child's usage of it. (11) Teach children to admire good English, because they imitate what they admire. (12) The child
should live in the atmosphere of good literature. Which is
better, to tell the story or to read it? (13) We do not real-
ly know a thing until it is given expression of some form. Recite, discuss and illustrate these principles. (14) The child
must take a genuine pleasure in his language work.

Lesson II.

Language Values.

1. Discuss the influence of the mother tongue as gotten
from the home and companions as affecting the work of the
school.

2. Show the value of language standards. Discuss good
literature as a means (1) in the composition exercises, (2)
in rhetoricals, (3) discuss the value of how and what to read.

3. Discuss the worth of copying, dictation, reproduction,
original exercises, training the ear to good English.

4. (1) Define grammar. (2) Trace this meaning
through the various exercises in grammar. (3) Determine

the intrinsic and relative values of defining, parsing, diagraming, rules, false syntax. (4) When would you teach punctuation, capitalization? (5) Should the illustrative sentence work be classed as a grammar or a composition exercise? What should be the subject matter of these sentences? (6) What is the value of transpositions?

5. Where in the course should the study of formal grammar begin?

6. Enumerate the values intrinsically and relatively in translating one form of English into another, one language into another.

7. Is there a language period? How do you account for the child learning words so rapidly? The accent of the mother tongue. Why is it difficult for old persons to recall names?

8. Upon what principle would you grade the work in language? Interest? Mental content? The difficulties involved? Stages of development? Season of the year?

Lesson III.

Language from the First to Fourth Grades Inclusive.

Talking.

1. Aims. (1) Freedom of expression controlled in the direction of consecutive arrangement of thought. (2) To train the ear, (a) to appreciate beautiful literature, (b) to detect gross errors, (c) to observe the oral sentence and oral paragraph. (3) To increase the child's vocabulary. (4) To lay the foundation for the written exercises that follow.

2. Forms and content. Impressive readings by teacher and pupil chosen from classic child literature. (2) Conversations on courteous forms of conduct, home and school life, pictures, festal days, topics from organized social life, current events of the community. (3) Stories from literature and history. (4) Selections memorized and recited. Make a list of topics suited to this class of exercise. Choose from the adopted text and other sources at your command, and arrange them according to the seasons.

3. Method. (1) Impressive oral reading. Use all the motives suggested in Lesson 1: vivid ideas especially tend to express themselves, social relations, imitation, pride in good reading, feeling a personal need, supplying some immediate

end. The teacher may read to the class, and members of the
class may read to each other and to (not for) the teacher.
The class should be a mutual admiration society reading-wise.
(2) Conversation.—Careful preparation on the part of the
teacher is required. Supply the environment to call forth the
spontaneous expression of the child along its own interests.
When he is going do not stop him. Let suggestions for correct usage come unconsciously. Gradually check all rambling
and irrelevant statements. But freedom is more important
than accuracy. What would be the result if you required a
finished product from the children? Fluency, accuracy and sequence should develop together. Explain. (3) Stories.—In
conversation the teacher suggests, supports and guides the
child, but to tell a complete story throws him upon his own
resources. The stories should first be read or told by the
teacher. Conversations upon them should follow, in a subsequent period to these exercises. Children are allowed to choose
stories to tell. (4) Memorizing,—First the selection should
be frequently read in order to arouse admiration. Second,
children are then allowed to choose what they wish to commit.
The committing, however, should be under the direction of the
teacher as far as possible. Third, the selections are recited,
not in a formal way, but in the social circle, each being made
to feel that he is contributing something to the occasion.

Writing.

1. Aim.—(1) To show in written form consecutive
thinking. (2) To capitalize, spell and punctuate correctly.
(3) To paragraph and show proper co-ordination and sub-
ordination by arrangement of the subject matter.

2. Content should be the same as for the oral exercises.

3. Method.—(1) Copying—First, transcribe script models; second, transcribe print into script; third, write memorized selections. Enumerate the benefits of copying. For the
first three years there should be little else but oral work.
Short, simple sentences should be copied and reproduced. The
first sentences should grow out of the reading lessons, pupils
making sentences for their fellows to read. Why should pupils be very exact in their writing? (2) Dictation.—Give
the values of dictation. There are two forms; the pupil dic-

tates to the teacher, the teacher dictates to the pupils. After the dictation compare the effort with the orignal and correct. Give the characteristics of good dictation. This should be a frequent exercise in the fourth grade especially. (3) Class composition.—The teacher places upon the board the sentences made by different members of the class. The result is a class composition. Seeing and sharing in thought and its expression is a powerful incentive to individual effort. The teacher must take care that the sentences must follow in proper order. Thus the oral paragraph leads to the written form. Pupils should copy the sentences as they are written. Point out the benefits of this exercise. (4) Dramatization.—This is also a class exercise. The story as told or read, dramatized and written on the board, copied by the pupils, committed and acted. In this manner let the members of the institute dramatize the "Three Bears." (5) Retelling Stories.—How does this differ from mere copying or repetition? Give an illustration to show how this work must be suited to the various grades. What class of material would you select? Give an illustrative lesson to the institute after the following outline: (a) One of the pupils reads the story aloud. (b) The teacher tells it, varying the language. (c) Questions are asked both by pupils and teachers. (d) One member of the class tells the story orally and the others criticize. (e) Write the story from memory. To call for more originality, change the point of view; if it be about animals, tell if about men. Transfer the scene to another locality; if told in first person tell it in the third, tell it about a classmate, etc. Use topical outlines sparingly. Why? (6) The use of pictures.—There are two classes of pictures, those that suggest a story and those that suggest description. The former class is to be used in these grades. The teacher should frequently describe a picture to show how. What are the objects to be secured in giving picture lessons? (7) Letter Writing.—As an original composition, why does letter writing stand first? Should first be a class exercise. What devices would you use to secure correct forms? (8) Correct Usage.—Correct errors in two ways, incidentally and by drills in correct forms. Usually incidental corrections are insufficient. It is necessary to drill upon correct forms under the stimulus of the strongest interest. Supplement the drills by providing occasion for the use of the correct forms in such a way that the child will feel the need of them.

LESSON IV.

Composition in the Grammar Grades.

Oral Composition—

1. *Aims.*—(1) To form ideals of good English and to enjoy them. (2) To take a pride in habitually conforming to these. (3) To organize one's thoughts and to express them in acceptable form without hesitation. (4) To increase the learner's vocabulary. (5) To furnish a motive for extended preparation and formal discourse. (6) To be versatile and inventive in expression. (7) To train one's self to be at ease in speaking in the presence of others.

2. Personal observation and researches supplementary to the text in use furnishes the content of this work. History, Literature, Geography, Nature Study abound in interesting material. Make a list of suitable subjects. It is important that every topic should have an educational value.

3. Methods.—(1) Reading. (a) Devise a method of approach that will arouse expectation. (b) Silently read the selection. (c) Tell it to the class in your own language. (d) To train the ear to good English read the selection in the best possible manner. (2) *Story Telling.*—Bring in information stories obtained from reading and retell them to the class. (3) *Recitation.*—Compare the value of the topic recitation with the question and answer method as to the language value. Special tasks assigned will give opportunity for an extended discourse. (4) *Arguments.*—The subject matter of geography and history may be thrown into the form of debate. Illustrate by giving many examples. (4) *Description and narration.*—Model descriptions and narrations should be read and their characteristics pointed out by the teacher. The pupil should then be required to imitate these, the objects and incidents being furnished by the teacher if need be.

Written Composition—

1. *Dictation.*—Study a well chosen selection as to capitals, punctuation, spelling and arrangement, and then write it from dictation. Write another from dictation without previous study and compare each member's effort with the original.

2. *Reproduction.*—Write from memory a poetic and a prose selection and compare it with the original. Read a description, a narration, and reproduce them in written form, using your own language.

3. *Letter Writing.*—One of the most useful and easy original exercises. After the form is taught as indicated in the text have the pupils write genuine letters. Enumerate the occasions for letters.

4. *Formal Composition.*—Let each member bring to the class his own contributions on the subject. After the subject has been thoroughly discussed the teacher directs in making an outline for the written form. How would you deal with these compositions after they are written? Show how current events may be used, written debates, etc.

5. *Examination.*—Train the pupils how to prepare creditable examination papers. Not only teach them how to arrange the work on the paper, but how to express themselves. Submit a set of questions and answer them as a class—the teacher guiding. In order to overcome the habit, of running statements together, have pupils (1) think the sentences before writing them, (2) express the thought independent of the language of the question, (3) first form the habit of making short sentences before trying their hand at the longer and the more difficult. Give an exercise, illustrating these suggestions.

LESSON V.

The authors of Graded Lessons in English speak of two classes of text books. Discuss these. In what grades is this text to be taught? What is the general plan? Why is the sentence chosen as the basis of presentation? What may be said of the disciplinary value of this method? How do the authors justify the use of so many detached sentences? What means do they use to teach the paragraph? Give the arguments for and against diagraming. Notice what the author classes as composition exercises. (1) Detached sentences, (2) analysis of selections from literature, (3) stories from pictures and current topics. The emphasis seems to be thrown upon the structure or form of oral and written composition, "how" as an object of knowledge rather than an actual system of practice. How would you supplement this deficiency? Two lessons in composition, as suggested above, if given in the right spirit, will do it. In what connections are the rules of capitals and punctuation marks taught in this text? Illustrate each of them.

LESSON VI.

Analyze and parse the following sentences: Lesson 65, Nos. 1, 3, 5, 8, 9, 12. Lesson 100, Nos. 1 to 11 inclusive. Let the exercise be illustrative of your method. How far would you follow the models for formal analysis and parsing? Discuss the value of oral and written analysis and parsing as such. Discuss the best plan for reviewing this text.

LESSON VII.

1. Illustrate the various uses of (1) the participle, (2) the phrase, (3) the clause. Be prepared to give the construction of the elements of each of these sentences.

2. Classify, define and illustrate sentences according to meaning and use. Let each sentence contain a historical or a geographical fact.

3. Diagram, analyze and parse the following sentences from Higher Lessons in English: Lesson 35, Nos. 4, 15; Lesson 42, Nos. 5, 12, 13; Lesson 47, No. 2; Lesson 48, Nos. 2, 8, 10; Lesson, 59, No. 9; Lesson 64, No. 8; Lesson 78, Nos, 8, 10; Lesson 80, Nos. 1, 5, 9, 13; Lesson 81, Nos. 6, 7, 9, 15; Lesson 145, No. 7.

LESSON VIII.

1. *False Syntax.*—Discuss the question of training the ear to correct forms. In what stage of advancement should false syntax be introduced for correction? Compare the method of dealing with these forms in the primary grades with that in the more advanced. The following sentences are correct. Read them aloud. Do they sound so?

It is we.
I thought it to be him.
How should you like to be I?
Whom is this for?
It is I who am offended.
He walks as I do.

Do you wish to lie on the sofa?
This is between him and her.
One knows one's own affairs best.
This dress sits well.
There is no use of his remaining.
He invited you and him.
I wish he would tell you and us.
I wish that I were going.
I saw him previously to his going.

2.   Three of the following ten sentences are correct. Justify your correction of the others.

I am so glad to meet you.
The goods are that wide.
I suppose he is offended.
I swum across the stream.
I lay on the sofa.
I had lain the carpet.
I have set here for an hour.
Come here and set your vase down and sit by my side.
I like to have my relatives for dinner.
He is never on time for his lesson.

3.   Make your choice of the words in parenthesis and then justify it.

The boat leaves (in on) time.
Come (in into) the house.
I am (apt liable) to forget.
I (gave donated) five dollars.
She goes twenty minutes (of to) five.
He lives (in at) Boston.
I (think guess) I shall return.
John lives a long (way ways) from here.
The wife and mother (was were) here.
Each was asked to give (his their) opinion.
I (live reside) on Central Avenue.
If I (was were) in the wrong I apologize.

4.   Write sentences containing "shall" and "will" denoting (1) simple futurity, (2) determination, (3) condition, (4) promise.

Lesson IX.

1. The authors teach the parts of speech in connection with analysis. The parts of speech are subdivided and the modifications of the parts of speech are considered as subsequent topics. What are the advantages of this mode of treatment? Is not this text too difficult for pupils of the eighth grade? In determining these lessons as such, what has been the motive? Has the amount of material or the unit of instruction been the determining factor? Make a list of the difficulties you have encountered in teaching this advanced book.

2. It is impossible to pass over as much ground in review as in the advanced work. There are three possible methods of reviewing. (1) Use questions to bring out the most salient points of the text. (2) Outline and recite from topics. (3) Supply new subject matter, calling for the pupil's knowledge of the subject. In harmony with these methods select a stanza, of poetry which will serve as a review and a test of one's knowledge of analysis. What cautions as to proper construction are the most difficult for you to understand and observe and apply? Be prepared to make every definition in the book plain by exposition and illustration. What plurals and declensions are the most difficult for you to remember? Make a list of the most troublesome irregular verbs.

Lesson X.

Prepare Lesson 81 of the text as you would have your pupils do. What determines the paragraph? Justify all the punctuation marks in the selections, Lesson 145.

Geography

1. The study of the North American continent from a complete outline. (See outline in "Methods and Aims in Geography," by Chas. F. King, quite complete.) Study this continent comparatively. Emphasize: Position, formation, size, topography, climate, animal and vegetable life, and the various industries. (Books of reference are listed at the end of these lessons.)

LESSON II.

1. Discuss the chief industries of North America.

2. What effect has elevation and distance from seaboard upon vegetable life and its distribution in North America?

3. Draw a map locating the zones, showing boundaries and width.

4. What is the fundamental law of the distribution of heat upon the surface of the globe; what modifications of this law are observable in North America?

5. Is there a general law that regulates the distribution of animal and vegetable life upon the globe, and how is this law related to the character and well being of the human family?

6. In what way is any portion of North America influenced for good or evil by winds or ocean currents?

7. Discuss the causes of the change of seasons.

8. Name and locate the races of mankind and give the distinguishing characteristics of each.

LESSON III.

1. What mountains or heights of land form the lake and river systems of the United States?

2. Discuss the United States from a complete outline (the one found on page 48 of King's Methods and Aims in Geography is a good one).

3. Discuss the principal river systems of the United States and show their importance.

4. Emphasize the following points of the outline: Position, surface, climate, life, productions, commerce, prominent cities and what led to their prominence.

5. Name the chief mining, manufacturing, commercial and agricultural centers of the United States and state for what each is noted.

6. Compare the United States in her great industries with France, Germany and England.

7. Contrast the educational advantages of the United States with those of France, Germany and England.

8. Compare climatic conditions of the United States with those of France, Germany and England.

Lesson IV.

1. What are the leading industries of New York and Pennsylvania as compared with Louisiana and Texas? What makes the difference in character of industries in the two sections? What has made great the cities of New York City, Philadelphia, New Orleans and Galveston?

2. Why have Chicago, Minneapolis, St. Louis, San Francisco, Denver and Kansas City, Missouri, become important centers in the United States?

3. Make a model study of the State of Ohio from a complete outline (the King outline is good). Emphasize strongly: Position, surface, drainage, climate, life, education, government, productions, industries, prominent cities, etc.

4. In what particular portions of the United States are the following commodities found in the greatest abundance: Lead, zinc, copper, iron, gold, silver, coal (anthracite), coal (bituminous), lumber, wool, wheat, corn, potatoes, rye, oats, hay, beans, beef, pork, cooton, sugar, rice, bananas, grapes, apples, peaches, pears, boots and shoes, clothing, carpets, farm machinery and household furniture.

5. Contrast the fruit growing industries of the Pacific coast with those of the Atlantic coast.

Lesson V.

1. Study California from a complete outline, emphasizing: Position, surface, drainage, climate, animal and vegetable life,

productions, industries, commerce and important cities.

2. Compare the conditions of California with those of Oregon and Washington—in what does each excel?

3. Sketch an outline map of Oregon, Washington, California, Idaho, Montana, Wyoming, Utah, Colorado, New Mexico and Arizona, showing location of mountains, rivers, deserts, etc.

4. What effect has the surface upon animal and vegetable life in this section.

5. Make a complete recitation on Canada from model outline, emphasizing the most important features of the outline.

6. Study Mexico from complete outline and contrast all conditions of position, surface, climate, productions, commerce, education, government, etc., with those of the United States.

Lesson VI.

1. Study South America from a complete outline as suggested on page 48 of King's "Methods and Aims in Geography."

2. Study comparatively with North America as to the following: Position, surface, drainage, political divisions, natural divisions, climate, animal and vegetable life, manners and customs, religion, education, government, production, industries, commerce and principal cities.

3. Name the political divisions of South America, and name and locate their capitals.

4. Describe Venezuela and her people.

5. Describe the State of Panama and the great project the United States is interested in there.

Lesson VII.

1. Sketch an outline map of Europe, locating the principal rivers, mountains, gulfs, bays, seas, cities and lakes.

2. Study comparatively with those of the United States the following conditions in Europe: Position, surface, drainage, politcal and natural divisions, climate, animal and vegetable life, population, races, language, manners and customs, education, religion, government, productions, industries, commerce, and principal cities.

3. State briefly for what each of the following cities is noted: Paris, Rome, Venice, Naples, Messina, Berlin, Vienna,

St. Petersburg, London, Liverpool, Constantinople, The
Hague, Copenhagen and Brussels.

4. Why is Great Britain a great commercial and manufacturing nation and how does it compare with the United
States in these particulars?

5. How do Great Britain and France compare in the
matter of industries, commerce, government, education, climate, productions and population?

Lesson VIII.

1. Sketch an outline map of Germany, locating its rivers,
mountains, capital, and principal cities.

2. What are the political divisions of Germany?

3. Describe the government of Germany, comparing it with
that of Russia.

4. Name the rulers of England, Germany and Russia.

5. Describe the chief industries of Germany—in what particulars do they excel all other nations?

6. Contrast the art, literature and science of Germany with
those of any other of the great nations.

7. What can you say of the great universities of Germany
and their influence upon the rest of the educational world?

8. Describe Holland and her people—their customs and
manners, industries, productions, climate, commerce, surface,
education, and population.

Lesson IX.

1. Contrast the people of China and Japan is to their
religion, government and civilization.

2. Why has Japan advanced and China remained at a
stand-still during the last half century?

3. What effect do the peculiar customs of China have upon
her advancement?

4. Describe the position of women in China.

5. Describe the system of education in that empire.

6. Describe the industries of China and Japan.

7. What effect has the surface, drainage and climate upon
the Chinese people?

8. What is meant by "the awakening of China?"

9. Describe India; its government, religion, surface, cli-

mate, productions. industries, population, cities. How does it compare with Japan.

LESSON X.

1. Study Africa from a complete outline, emphasizing position, surface, drainage and climate.
2. Contrast Africa with South America on the above four points.
3. Why is it that the great inland lakes and the great rivers of Africa have not proved a great blessing to that continent?
4. Is there any meaning to the term "Darkest Africa"?
5. Give cause and effect of the great Desert of Africa.
6. What European colonies have been planted in Africa, and how have they prospered?
7. Describe the Congo State and tell of its government and people.
8. What can you say of the "Boers"?
9. Compare the civilization, surface, drainage, climate, industries and people of Africa with those of Australia.
10. Contrast the animal and vegetable life of those two continents.

Books of Reference.

Natural Introductory Geography, Hinman.
Geographical Readers, Carpenter.
Rivers of North America, Russell.
Aspects of the Earth, Shaler.
The Earth and Man, Guyot.
Physical Geography, Guyot.
The People's Natural History.
Great Races of Mankind, Redpath.
Natural School of Geography, Hinman.
This Continent of Ours, King.
Reports of the Commissioner of Education.
Methods of Teaching Geography, King.
Stoddard's Lectures.
Commercial Geography, Adams.
Comparative Geography, Ritter.
Rise and Development of Japan, Smith.

Reading

Necessity for a more decided interest to be taken in teaching reading. How may a pupil be taught to get a clear idea of the *mechanics* of Reading? What is the relative importance of *thought* getting in Reading? Should a teacher have an appreciation of the meaning and beauty of literature in order to teach Reading successfully? Is the vocal expression of the pupil stimulated when he desires to impress upon others the beauty and feeling that impressed him?

What prepaartion should a teacher have made before attempting to *teach* Reading in our public schools? What is meant by a Reading recitation?

(Books of reference are listed at the end of these lessons Sherman and Reed's "Essentials of Teaching Reading" is the basis of this course.)

LESSON II.

How is the element, *Time,* to be taught to the average pupil? How are pupils to be made to feel the grandeur of the twenty-third psalm? Of the Battle Hymn of the Republic? Of Lincoln's Gettysburg speech? To what extent do the emotions enter into thought-getting and vocal expression?

Why did the war correspondents fail to sing the last stanza of "The Battle Hymn of the Republic"? What determines the fastness or slowness of the rate in Reading? What is meant by "largeness of thought" in Reading? How should the first chapter of Genesis be read? Commit the first stanza or paragraph of "The Rainy Day," by Longfellow, and the "Recessional," by Kipling. What is the purpose of the recitation?

LESSON III.

Why do good readers divide the words of selections they read into groups? What determines the words that belong in any particular group? Can rules be given for grouping?

Commit to memory the first and seventh stanzas of "The Village Blacksmith" and show how the words should be grouped. What exercises train children to group? How should the words in the following stanzas be grouped? How read?

"The day is dark and cold and dreary,
It rains and the wind is never weary,
The vine still clings to the mouldering wall.
And at each blast the dead leaves fall.
The day is dark and dreary."

"How dear to my heart are the scenes of my childhood,
When fond recollections present them to view,
The orchard, the meadow, the deep tangled wildwood,
And every loved spot which my infancy knew."

How is it possible for a teacher to make the teaching and reading so interesting that *all* the pupils will enjoy the lessons? What are the essentials of a recitation?

Lesson IV.

What is the function of melody in reading or speaking? What is meant by the main idea in a sentence and how is this to be determined? How may children be taught to find the main idea? In reading or speaking, when does emphasis manifest itself in a child's language? Of what importance is this element? How should emphasis and melody be taught in the following selections:

"Among the beautiful pictures
That hang on memory's wall,
Is one of a dim old forest
That seemeth best of all."

"How often, oh, how often,
In the days that had gone by,
I stood on that bridge at midnight
And gazed on that wave and sky."

"How often, oh, how often,
I had wished that the ebbing tide
Would bear me away on its bosom
O'er the ocean, wild and wide."

Would you require the boy, whose voice is changing, to attempt the above selections? Who should criticize the reader of the selection? If the pupil is timid, awkward and peculiarly modest, how best get his confidence? When should the teacher read the selection for the pupil?

"*Preparation for the Recitation; or the Art of Study,*" by Hamilton: How may a teacher profit by the study of Chapter IV of the above book?

LESSON V.

How does force manifest itself in the mind of the speaker or reader? State specifically the differences that exist in reading, declaiming and acting. What is the function of force? Of what psychological condition is force the result? Illustrate the different kinds of force by the following:

Down, down, your lances, down.
Bear back both friend and foe.

Leave the room, sir.
Carry-Arms. Present Arms. Halt.

O, sing unto the Lord a new song.
Sing unto the Lord all the earth.

"God give us men. A time like this demands
Strong minds, great hearts, true faith and ready hands,
Men whom the lust of office does not kill;
Men whom the spoils of office cannot buy;
Men who possess opinions and a will;
Men who have honor ; men who will not lie;
Men who can stand before a demagogue
And damn his treacherous flatteries, without winking;
Tall men sun crowned, who live above the fog
In public duty and in private thinking."

Study the psychology of Stress and Force in order to criticize justly. If the recitation in reading tests, teaches, or trains, and the learner acquires knowledge, power, or skill, then how best conduct the recitation in order that the above ends may be secured?

Lesson VI.

What does the quality of the voice of a speaker indicate? Can the speaker control the quality of his voice? What is meant by the orotund quality of voice? When should it be used? What is meant by the guttural quality of the voice and when should it be used? What is the aspirated quality and when used?

Upon what psychological conditions are the various qualities of the voice dependent? What is meant by the *atmosphere* of the selection? What can a teacher do to assist the pupil in getting the atmosphere of any particular selection? Illustrate the different qualities of the voice by the following selections: *"The Village Blacksmith"; Poe's "The Raven"; Gray's elegy"; Lincoln's Gettysburg Speech; "The Chariot Race, by Lew Wallace; "The September Gale," by Holmes; "Snowbound," by Whittier.*

Study critically Chapter II of Hamilton's "Recitation."

Lesson VII.

What care should be used in the assignment of a Reading lesson for any grade in the public schools? What preliminary work should be done by the teacher in order that pupils may get the correct pronunciation and meanings of all words and the correct interpretation of all allusions, whether of an historical, Biblical or other character? What particular attention should be given to articulation and what drills may be used to give good articulation? What is the value of supplementary reading and how should it be used? What would be a model assignment for *Paul Revere's Ride,* page 187 of Sherman and Reed's text?

Study carefully Chapter III, Hamilton's "Recitation."

Lesson VIII.

Discuss the following methods of teaching Reading and state upon what principles each is founded: The Alphabet, Phonic, Word, Sentence, and Eclectic.

What should be the foundation principles for teaching primary Reading? Of what importance to the child is a *desire* to read and how may the teacher strengthen this feeling? How much time should be devoted to phonics? How may a child be taught to use the dictionary? In what grade should the analysis of words begin? What is the psychological condition of the child's mind when an attempt is made to dramatize some of the simpler selections with which the children are familiar?

Study carefully Chapters IV, V, and VI of Hamilton's "Recitation."

Lesson IX.

What are some of the most marked defects in the reading as taught in our public schools and how may these be remedied? Name some of the obstacles that must be overcome in order to get good results in teaching reading. Children often have wrong ideals concerning reading when they enter school; how may these be supplanted by good ones?

What is the strongest incentive to a child that he may do his best when reading a selection? Is it poossible for a teacher to eliminate the self-consciousness of a pupil while he is reading? What does it mean for a child to read intelligently, intelligibly, forcefully and gracefully? How may each of the above conditions be realized?

Study carefully Chapter VII of Hamilton's "Recitation."

Lesson X.

Make a moled assignment for "Lochinvar" (page 184, Sherman and Reed's text) or "Barbara Fritchie," (page 185, Sherman and Reed's text).

Read the selection and discuss the various phases of Time, Grouping, Melody, Force, and Quality.

References,

Essentials of Teaching Reading, Sherman and Reed.
How to Teach Reading, S. H. Clark.
The Recitation, Hamilton.
Some Good Psychology.

Physiology

Lesson I.

1. Why should teachers study the principles of Hygiene?
2. Define Anatomy and Physiology.
3. What is the purpose of foods? Make an outline, classifying the different kinds.
4. Name and locate the organs of digestion and make a drawing of the stomach.
5. Explain the purpose of the following fluids: Saliva, chyme, chyle, pancreatic and intestinal juices, bile.
6, Explain what is meant by oxidation in the body.
7. Is health a civic obligation?
8. How may teachers improve health conditions in a school and in the community?
9. Why is it best to preach health from the standpoint of industrial and national efficiency rather than of individual well-being?
10. Does the failure to enforce health laws result in a menace to the general health of a community?

Lesson II.

1. Discuss how plants live and grow. Relation of plants to animals. Plant digestion and plant food.
2. How should food be prepared for the human stomach?
3. What is meant by appetite and when is it natural?
4. Is the desire for stimulants or narcotics a natural one?
5. What positive position should a teacher take in reference to the use of narcotics or stimulants by the pupils?
6. What effect does the use of these have on the physical and moral nature?
7. What special pleading should be made for temperance in all things?
8. Discuss the seven health motives and seven catchwords suggested in "Civic and Health," by Allen.

LESSON III.

1. What is the function of the blood, its composition? How is it nourished? Use of the different kinds of corpuscles. Describe the plasma. Function of blood clotting.

2. Make a drawing of the heart, locating all valves, etc.

3. Describe the spleen. Its use.

4. Effect of too violent exercise upon the heart.

5. Evil effects of alcoholic stimulants or narcotics on the heart.

6. Describe complete circulation of the blood, naming all organs passed through.

7. What simple experiments may be introduced by the teacher to show the composition of the blood?

8. What health rights are not enforced in your community?

9. Can contagious and infectious diseases be prevented?

10. How may a teacher assist in the matter of keeping a disease from spreading?

LESSON IV.

1. Describe the lungs and make a drawing of the same Give the specific function of the lungs.

2. Define respiration.

3. What properties are exhaled from, or inhaled into, the body by the action of the lungs and what effect do these have upon the blood?

4. What is the necessity for complete ventilation in our school rooms?

5. Explain some good plans for ventilating.

6. Necessity for the correct heating of our school rooms.

7. Necessity for the correct lighting of the same.

8. Is the physical welfare of children an index to community health?

9. Should there be a physical examination of children by a competent person at the beginning of each term?

10. What is the difference between a medical examination and a medical inspection?

LESSON V.

1. Make an outline of the skeleton.

2. Give uses and composition of the bones.

3. What care should be taken with children in order that they may have well formed bones?

4. Describe the muscles of the body; their function.

5. What is meant by training the muscles?

6. How may a strong, muscular system be developed?

7. Describe the joints; their uses.

8. Describe the tendons; their uses.

9. What effect has healthful exercise on the bones and muscles?

10. What evil effects do alcoholic stimulants have upon the muscular system?

LESSON VI.

1. Make a drawing of the kidneys and give their function.

2. Describe the structure of the skin; care of same. Its function.

3. Necessity for cleanliness. Proper kind of baths.

4. How should a body be clothed in order to secure good health?

5. What efforts should a teacher make that she may train her pupils to care for the kidneys and skin that no diseases may follow as a result of confinement in the school room?

6. Discuss "mouth breathing."

7. Discuss the effects of adenoids.

8. Can teachers train children to guard against "catching" cold? How?

9. Can a teacher suggest methods of a precautionary character that would tend to prevent children or communities from catching communicable or transmissible diseases?

LESSON VII.

1. Why should a teacher take a most positive stand against the use of stimulants and narcotics?

2. In what way does our nation suffer economically, morally and spiritually from their use?

3. Tell of the evil effects of alcohol in county, state, and nation.

4. Evils arising from the use of tobacco.

5. The evil of the cigarette.

6. What simple experiments may a teacher make to show

the evil effects of alcohol on the organs of the body or the effect of narcotics upon the same?

7. How may a teacher learn to know infectious and contagious diseases? (Pages 64 and 65 "Civics and Health.")

8. What should be done with children having such diseases?

9. Should the teacher insist on "compulsory vaccination"?

10. Should the teacher and physician work in harmony? ("Civics and Health," pp. 268-282.)

Lesson VIII.

1. What is meant by the nervous system, and upon what does a good, strong system depend?

2. Make a drawing of the brain.

3. Describe the functions of the medulla oblongata, cerebellum, cerebrum and spinal cord.

4. Describe the nerves, structure and uses.

5. What is the importance of habit and its effect in forming correct modes of living?

6. What effect have pleasant and agreeable surroundings in the school room upon the nervous system of the child?

7. What effect have evil companions upon the nervous system of the average child?

8. Does kindly treatment in the home and school beget a stable nervous system? Why?

9. What effect does the use of tobacco have upon the nerves of the boy?

10. Effect of alcohol upon the nervous system?

Lesson IX.

1. Make a drawing of the eye, showing the various parts and giving their functions and structure.

2. Name some of the defects of the eye and tell how they may be remedied.

3. What is the proper care of the eye?

4. Describe the human ear; name its parts and its functions.

5. Care of the ear.

6. Describe the organs of taste and smell.

7. What ill results come from "eye strain"?

8. How may a teacher assist in relieving this condition?

9. What eye tests are possible for a teacher to make?

10. When should a teacher suggest to parents that they have the eyes of their children examined by competent physicians?

Lesson X.

1. Why is sanitation one of the important themes in our school system at this time?

2. Upon what does good health largely depend?

3. Is it a fact that disease is the result of the violation of the laws of health?

4. What diseases are contagious?

5. What is meant by bacteria?

6. How are diseases communicated in the public schools?

7. Necessity for pure drinking water.

8. Necessity of good ventilation.

9. Can the nervousness of teacher and pupil be reduced to a minimum? How?

10. Why is "play" so beneficial to children?

11. What effect upon the school has the health of a teacher?

12. Do habits of health promote industrial efficiency? ("Civics and Health," pp. 209-228.)

References.

1. Elementary Physiology, Conn.
2. Applied Physiology, Overton.
3. Human Body, Martin.
4. Town and City, Gulick.
5. Control of Body and Mind, Gulick.
6. Good Health, Gulick .
7. Anatomy, Gray.
8. Bacteria and Their Products, Woodhead.
9. Bacteria, Newman.
10. Bacteria, Yeases and Moulds in the Home, Conn.
11. Civics and Health, Allen.
12. World's Temperance, Craft.

History

Lesson I.

1. Discuss early voyages of the Northmen.
2. Trials and tribulations of Columbus.
3. What explorations were made by Spain, France and England before the middle of the 17th century? What motives prompted each?
4. Describe the American Indian and tell why he has not made greater progress?
5. What is meant by a good method of teaching History?
6. Outline a good method for such teaching.
7. Why should biography be the basis for all primary history teaching?
8. How should maps be used in teaching history?
9. What preparation ought a teacher to make before attempting to teach history?
10. Name a list of good books on history that would furnish supplementary and collateral material for class use.

(Books for reference are listed at the end of these lessons.)

Lesson II.

1. State briefly the main circumstances as to time, place, and purpose of the settlements made by the Spanish, Dutch, French and English on the North American Continent.
2. In what ways are the lives and characters of the following men connected with the growth and development of the American Colonies:

Roger Williams, William Penn, James Oglethorpe, John Smith, Peter Stuyvesant, Lord Baltimore, George Carteret, and John Winthrop.

3. Discuss the differences of manners, customs and industries of the Dutch, French and English colonies.
4. Discuss Miles Standish as a type of pilgrim.
5. Discuss La Salle as a type of missionary.
6. Discuss King Philip as a type of Indian.

LESSON III.

1. Give a model outline for the study of the Virginia Colony.

2. Sketch an outline map of the thirteen Colonies.

3. What influence did the Puritans, Quakers and the Cavaliers have upon the character of the early settlers in the Colonies?

4. Contrast the economic and social conditions of the north, middle and the south groups of the Colonies.

5. Contrast the educational development in the same.

. 6. (a) Discuss Gov. Winthrop as a type of Puritan.

(b) Discuss Lord Baltimore as a type of statesman.

(c) Discuss Roger Williams as a type of missionary.

(d) Discuss William Penn as a type of Quaker.

(e) Discuss Washington as a type of soldier.

7. Who were some of the great men that Virginia produced and of what service have they been to their country?

LESSON IV.

1. Give causes and results of the French and Indian wars.

2. Were the motives of the French and English the same in the matter of colonization?

3. What was the principal cause of the American Revolution?

4. What did the Americans gain by the war?

5. Mention the most important statesman and the most important soldier of Revolutionary times and give a reason for your judgment. -

6. In what way were the following men of service to the Colonies: Patrick Henry, Samuel Adams, Lafayette and Benj. Franklin.

7. What were some of the educational institutions founded in the colonies before our constitutional history began, and what has been their influence?

8. Why had there been religious disturbances in the Colonies prior to the adoption of the Constitution?

LESSON V.

1. When and where did the Continental Congresses meet, and what action was taken in each of these meetings?

2.   Describe in detail the "Declaration of Independence."

3.   Describe the "Articles of Confederation" and tell why they did not prove satisfactory.

4.   Describe the origin of the present Constitution.

5.   What can you say of the character of the framers of the Constitution?

6.   Why was it necessary that compromises should be made in framing the constitution?

7.   How was the Constitution ratified?

8.   Early financial difficulties; how met?

9.   Discuss the early tariff laws.

10.   Discuss the organization of the National Bank.

11.   In what ways were the following men identified with the early Constitutional history of our country: George Washington, John Hancock, Thomas Jefferson, John Adams. Alexander Hamilton and Gouverneur Morris.

Lesson VI.

1.   What trouble did the United States have with France at the beginning of our Constitution period?

2.   Explain the Milan and Berlin decrees of Napoleon.

3.   Explain Orders in Council of England.

4.   Explain the Embargo of Jefferson.

5.   What was the final outcome of the commercial reprisals on the part of France, England and the United States?

6.   Give causes and results of the War of 1812.

7.   What gave rise to the Holy Alliance?

8.   What gave rise to the Monroe Doctrine?

9.   What was the Ashburton treaty?

10.   What led to the annexation of Texas?

11.   What caused the war with Mexico?

Lesson VII.

1.   State the boundaries of the thirteen original states after the treaty of 1783.

2.   What territory was relinquished to the common union by the original states?

3.   State from whom, when and how (whether by purchase, conquest, annexation, or treaty) the several additions to the United States have been obtained: Louisiana, Florida, Texas, Oregon Territory, California and New Mexico, Gadsden Pur-

chase, Alaska, Hawaian Islands, Porto Rico, Guam, Tutuila.

4. Has our nation become a world power?

LESSON VIII.

1. What were the main causes of the Civil War?

2. What were the compromises that were made from time to time that prevented for a time the conflict that was bound to come?

3. In what way were the following men identified with the main cause of the War of Secession: Wilmot, Clay, Calhoun, Taney, Webster, Seward, Garrison, Douglas, Sumner Greeley, Lincoln?

4. What was the Dred Scott Decision? Its effect?

5. Kansas-Nebraska Act? Its effect?

6, Secession of the Southern States?

7. Result of the Civil War?

8. What amendments were made to the constitution as a result of the war?

LESSON IX.

1. Describe the Public Land Grants in this country.

2. What events have stimulated the growth of commerce?

3. What effect have the thousands of inventions in labor-saving machinery had upon our nation?

4. Describe five of the most important inventions and tell why so important.

5. Describe the growth of the protection theory in our country and tell its effect.

6. Why has our nation made treaties of reciprocity with other nations?

7. What financial crises have occurred in our country and what were their causes?

8. Describe the Public Land Grants to New Mexico and her institutions under the act admitting New Mexico to statehood.

9. What are other general provisions to the statehood bill admitting New Mexico?

LESSON X.

1. Why should the teacher of history keep in touch with current events?

2. Describe the Ballinger-Pinchot trouble.

3. What recent change has taken place in the National "House of Representatives"?

4. What prominent private citizens have been away for the past several months and how were they received in foreign countries?

5. What historic meeting of chief executives occurred within the past year?

6. What are some of the main bills passed by the late Congress?

7. Name the principal leaders in Congress of the Republicans and Democrats.

8. What labor disturbances occurred in the United States during the past year?

9. What about the Nicaragua affair?

Books of Reference.

Leading Facts in American History, Montgomery.

The Northmen, J. E. Olson.

Guide to American History, Channing and Hart.

The Colonies, R. G. Thwaite.

How to Study and Teach History, Hinsdale.

Discovery of America, John Fiske.

The American Indian as a Product of Environment, A. J. Fynn.

Era of Colonization, Hart.

Building of the Republic, Hart.

National Expansion, Hart.

The Recitation, Hamilton.

New France and New England, Fiske.

The American Revolution, Fiske.

The American Revolution, Lecky.

Formation of the Union, Hart.

The Confederation and the Constitution, McLaughlin.

Division and Reunion, Woodrow Wilson.
Welding of the Nation, Hart.
Louisiana Purchase, Hosmer.
Expansion, Strong.
National Development, Sparks.
Ohio and Her Western Reserve, Matthews.
American Nation as a World Power, Latane.
American Territorial Development, Caldwell.
Steps in the Expansion of Our Territory, Austin.
The Purchase of Alaska, Austin.
Problems in Expansion, Whitelaw Reid.
Parties and Slavery, Smith.
Causes of the Civil War, Chadwick.
Outcome of the Civil War, Hosmer.
Civil War and the Constitution, Burgess.
Reconstruction and the Constitution, Burgess.
Reminiscences of the Civil War, Gordon.
Slavery and Abolition, Hart.
National Problems, Dewey.
History of the United States, McMaster.
History of the United States, Woodrow Wilson.

Civics

Lesson I.

1. Describe the local government in the Colonies prior to the Revolution.

2. What is government and why is there a necessity for the same?

3. Define and illustrate theocratic, monarchial, aristocratic, and republican forms of government.

4. Compare the formation of the Roman government with that of the English government.

5. What is a constitution.

6. It has been said that the "Magna Charta," "Bill of Rights" and "Petition of Rights" are the corner stones of the American Constitution. Why?

Lesson II.

1. What different views as to the form of government that should prevail were in existence in the colonies prior to 1775?

2. What influence did such men as Otis, Henry, Lee, and Samuel Adams have in crystalizing a strong sentiment towards self-government in the colonies?

3. Describe the New England Confederation.

4. Describe the "Albany Plan."

5. When and where were Continental Congresses held? State results of each.

6. In what way were the following men connected with the establishment of the fundamental law of the United States: Washington, Hamilton, Jefferson, John Adams, Franklin, Madison and Henry?

Lesson III.

1. What were the Articles of Confederation, and what were their defects?

2. Why was a constitution proposed to supplant the Articles of Confederation?

3. Give the preliminary steps taken to organize a Constitutional Convention.

4. State time, place and character of the men who formed the convention.

5. Why was it necessary to make compromises? Name the most important ones made.

6. How was the constitution ratified?

7. What provision was embodied in the fundamental law that enables the people to change the same?

LESSON IV.

1. The Legislative Department is how comprised?

2. House of Representatives: Organization, members, election, qualifications and disqualifications; steps taken in apportionment; gerrymandering and its remedy; contests; vacancies; organizing powers; election of officers and adopting rules and appointment of committees; compensation in salary; perquisites; privileges; judicial powers—seat, punish, and expel members, impeach officers, delegates from territories.

3. Senate: Organization; members—numbers, election, term, qualifications and disqualifications; contests, relation to the state; vacancies; presiding officers; organizing powers—officers, rules, committes; compensation; privileges; judicial powers—seat, punish, and expel members and try impeachments; executive powers—treaties, appointments.

4. Outline the powers of Congress.

5. Discuss the following powers: Taxation, money, revenue, commerce, naturalization, postoffice and post roads, war.

6. What is the meaning of the following: Habeas Corpus, Bill of Attainder, and Ex Post Facto? What is the limitation upon Congress in reference to them?

LESSON V.

1. Describe the different ways whereby a bill may become a law.

2. Who are the presiding officers of the House of Representatives and the Senate? What authority have they?

3. What is meant by a quorum?

4. What is filibustering and its effect upon legislation?

5. What special executive powers does the Senate possess?

6. Give the complete process of naturalization.

7. How are amendments made to the Constitution? (Be specific.)

8. Describe the following: Meetings of Congress and ways of adjournment; long, short and special sessions; committee work; joint and conference committees; calendar; process in passage of a bill; ways of voting.

LESSON VI.

1. Discuss the following: The President; term; qualification; eligibility; vacancy; law of succession; compensation; powers—diplomatic, treaties, foreign agents, legislative, special session, adjournment, message, veto, promulgation of laws, military commander-in-chief, war officers; judicial powers—appointment of judges, pardons, reprieves.

2. Discuss the cabinet officers and name the present body. Duty of each cabinet officer. Name the principal bureaus under each.

LESSON VII.

1. Of what shall the Supreme Court of the United States consist?

2. Name the members of the present Supreme Court.

3. Discuss the following: Tenure, term and compensation, division of courts, supreme, circuit, court of appeals, district, territorial, claims, District of Columbia, equity, diplomatic and colonial courts.

4. Powers of courts; character of subject matter; character of parties. Distribution of these powers: original and appellate jurisdiction; limitation of authority.

LESSON VIII.

1. Legislative department of New Mexico: the two houses, the members, number in each house, qualifications, election, term of office, privileges, compensation, sessions; journal: yeas and nays.

2. Suffrage; qualifications of voters; who not qualified; taxations, exemptions, etc.

3. Describe the Department of Education of New Mexico, name the officers and give their duties.

4. Name and locate the state Educational Institutions of

Mexico and what is the particular function of each individual school?

5. Name and locate the territorial asylums, hospitals and the penitentiary of New Mexico.

6. What is the power and duty of the Constitutional Convention?

7. How is the Constitution to be ratified?

Lesson IX.

1. Give the names of the executive officers of New Mexico.

2. Name the judiciary for New Mexco.

3. What is a state constitution, and how does it differ from the national constitution?

4. Give the duties of each Territorial officer, compensation and term of office.

5. Contrast the early local governments of New England with those of the Southern colonies.

6. Give the evolution and growth of township, city and county governments in the United States.

7. Discribe city and county governments in New Mexico and name the officers and give duties of the principal officers in each.

Lesson X.

1. Discuss the Public Land Grants for New Mexico, the bill admitting New Mexico to statehood.

2. Relation of State and Nation; forms guaranteed; treaties, war, letters of marque and reprisal; money; police powers; return of crimnals; protection of aliens; admission of states, method, limitations.

3. The first ten amendments to the Constitution are called the American Bill of Rights; what privileges and immunities are guaranteed to the people of the country by these amendments?

4. What amendments to the Constitution of the U. S. are now being submitted to the several states of the Union for ratification?

5. What particular reciprocity treaties has the United States made within the past year?

References

1. School Civics, Boynton.
2. The Federalist, Madison.
3. The Constitution, Story.
4. Civics, Fiske.
5. Civics, Hinsdale.
6. Civics, Andrews.
7. Actual Government, Hart.

Elements of Pedagogy

These outlines are based upon Hamilton's "The Recitation" (Lippincott, Philadelphia) and the writer's review of it in the New Mexico Journal of Education. He urges that each member of the Institute receive the paper and the text and come to the meetings of the institute fully prepared to discuss both the topics and the questions raised under them.

There are two methods of presenting a subject more or less familiar to teachers: The concentric and the thorough-going. The concentric method takes a slice from one general feature of the subject after another, returning, after taking each in order, to the first selected; thus making round after round, each turn cutting deeper and deeper into the meaning. The thorough-going method takes up each topic in order, also, but treats it exhaustively before leaving it for another. The first plan is the method for the child and the beginner. The second is the one employed by our text. It takes for granted that the student is more or less informed on pedagogy and is fully able to appreciate the profounder views of the subject.

We plan then that the discussion follow this second method and take up each topic in succession. Work the field systematically and thoroughly. You cannot cover the course in the allotted time. This can be done either by your own efforts or at some future time at institute or summer school.

Lesson I.

(The Recitation in General.)

Thoroughly discuss the following topics: (1) Nature.—Define the recitation and distinguish it from learning. What are the senses in which this term has been used? (2) Discuss it as a two-fold process—teaching, learning. (3) Show its importance as affecting the pupils thinking, study and taste for learning. (4) Characteristics of a good recitation as to time, rate, order, intensity, adaptability, completeness, and clearness of thought. (5) What are the author's indictments against the average recitation?

LESSON II.

1. *Purpose.*—What is the effect of the aim on the method and the means? Discuss the importance of preparing for the recitation. What is the effect of the aim on the effort? Compare the aims of the pupil and the teacher. Discuss and classify aims. Arrange educational aims according to their importance or relative values.

2. *Essentials of the Recitation.*—What are the essentials of the recitation? Why so called? How are interest and attention related to the aims of teaching, such as knowledge? *Interest.*—Define interest. Interest may arise from the nature of the idea or things. It may arise from the relations of the ideas or things. In the former case it is natural, in the latter, acquired. Inherent and associated, direct and indirect, intrinsic and extrinsic are other terms which one may use to make the same distinction. In view of these distinctions, compare the interest of the miser and the spendthrift; home and foreign geography; three times four in view of its immediate use, and as it is presented to the child in the multiplication table. Compare the child that is interested as to his susceptibilies to instruction and management to one who is not. There are two forms of acquired interest; that which comes from those ideas or experience that are essentially related and that which arises from those which may be artificially related. There are three phases of the first form: (1) The interest that is awakened by discerning the new in the old. (2) The interest awakened by discerning the old in the new. (3) The useful. Give illustrations of each of these. The teacher appeals to the artificial interest when he offers a reward for study. The child is interested in the reward rather than in the subject itself. Prizes, immunities, and privileges all fall under this class of interest or incentivies. Can all knowledge be made inherently and essentially attractive? Should the pupil be induced to work for grades and head marks? If the child is not interested in school, whose fault is it?

LESSON III.

(Essentials Continued—Attention.)

1. How are interest and attention related? Show the necessity of attention in teaching. What is meant by the inattentive pupil? When the teacher has lost the attention of her class what does it indicate? Define attention. Two things determine the degree of attention: (1) The amount of available nervous energy. (2) The strength of the stimuli.

2. Three stages in the development of attention How does it come that the mind focuses itself upon an idea or object of perception? (1) The mind, spontaneously, as the plant gropes for the light, turns inherently to the strongest stimulus. This is the primary or child's attention .(2) But the strongest stimulus is not always to be followed. The development of the individual requires that he control his actions in reference to remote rather than immediate ends. His accumulating experiences soon teach him that it is to his best interest to often resist the strongest stimulus for the weaker one. This originates inhibition of effort, a battle against nature. It is this battle that gives us strength, that makes development possible. This is the controlled attention, the product of culture and civilization. (3) The third stage in the development of attention has been reached when the voluntary form becomes no longer an effort; when the duty becomes a pleasure; when work becomes play. What is the difference between work and play?

Discuss the pedagogy of attention after the following outline. (1) Favorable and unfavorable conditions for attention. (2) Inherent powers of the teacher to secure attention (3) How not to secure attention. (4) How to secure attention. (5) How to hold it when once secured.

LESSON IV.

(Parts of the Recitation.)

1. *Testing.*—What are the objects of tests? Compare oral and written tests. How would you grade oral topical responsions? Do you see any gain when teaching and testing follow each other in quick succession? In the formal separation? Why do teachers confuse testing and teaching? What should determine how often tests should be given?

2. *Teaching.*—What is meant by teaching? Compare the activities of the teacher and the pupil. Compare the favorable attitudes of mind of both. Definitions, expositions, explanations, suggestions, questions used as means to arouse pupils to activity. Using pupil's own knowledge from which he must do his own thinking. Define teaching. Discuss the question and answer method. If each pupil feels free to contribute something, how do you keep out the irrelevant?

3. *Training.*—Discuss the nature of habit and show its relation to training. Enumerate equivalent terms. Discuss the objects of training. Show that the early training of children precedes instruction. Discuss training after the following outline: (1) Practice makes perfect. (2) We learn to do by doing. (3) Adapting the practice to the child. (4) Diligent practice vs. routine drill. Enumerate six advantages secured by drills.

4. *Assignment.*—Think what is meant by assignment in the various grades. (1) Time to make the assignment. (2) Extent of the assignment. (3) Character of efficient assignment. How much time would you take for the assignment. What would you consider an unpedagogical assignment?

LESSON V.

1. *Importance of Study.*—Distinguish thinking from rote learning. Value of all teaching is measured by being a means to stimulate thought. What is it to think? What is it to study? Give the etymological definition of study. What is meant by thorough study? Would you expect study from pupils of all grades?

2. *Possiblities of Study.*—The possibilities for study arise from three sources: From a world of related things, the constitution of the mind itself, from a favorable relation of the two. Show that the world is a system of related things. This gives rise to what activities of the mind? What is an original thinker? What is meant by progressive thinking? Define and illustrate science. Can you show the advantages of the educated man in thinking a given process of any kind?

3. *Conditions for Effective Study.*—(1) Discuss the physical conditions, temperature, pure air, quietude, habit, etc. (2) Mind conditions. Interest.—What are the various forms of interest? Enjoyment in study. Is it possible to make all

branches equally interesting? Discuss the two kinds of interest. Contrast reflective and objective study. Ability to study—another requisite. Pupils must have the power to concentrate the mind—must be able to relate truth. Discuss fully the question of lack of ability of pupils, as one of the problems of the school.

4. *Objects of Study.*—(1) Well formed mind.—Distinguish general and special discipline. Discuss the doctrine of formal discipline. Independent effort. How much help would you give a student? Under what conditions would you allow partnership study? (2) A well filled mind. (3) Character.— What is it. Enumerate elements of character developed by right study.

(5)) *Stages of Study.*—Explain the three stages of study —(1) Apprehension, (2) Comprehension, (3) Application.

LESSON VI.

(Method of Study.)

1. How not to study. Discuss the counterfeit methods of study.

2. Common and special methods of study. Show the nature of general methods of study. How far would you influence the child's mode of study?

3 State and discuss these rules for study: (1) Thoughtful reading. (2) Outlining. (3) Reflective repetition. (4) Inference. (5) Verification. (6) Character.

4. What to do with the unprepared. (1) Remove the cause. (2) Do not hear an unprepared lesson. (3) Prepare pupils before or in a study recitation. (4) Be sure to have the attention of the class. (5) Insist upon a study program.

LESSON VII.

(Explain Steps—Inductive Teaching.)

Explain the long drawn out thinking processes of induction and deduction—how the general is discovered and confined— the concrete and the abstract. Briefly explain and define the five formal steps. Show how knowledge advances.

1. *Preparation.*—What is its function? (1) Formal preparation a necessity. (2) Must be appropriate. Explain

how lesson units are connected. Explain the principles—"From the known to the unknown."—"From the simple to the complex." Illustrate these fully. Show how the new may be approached from several avenues.

2. *Presentation.*—What are the various ways of presenting the new? Give its purpose. External characteristics of successful presentation: (1) Clearness—which requires that the teacher have a clear idea of what he wishes to present, and then must express this idea in simple, direct language. (2) Presentation must have strength—this requires clearness, earnestness, and repetition. (3) It must be logical. What enables a teacher to present a lesson logically? (4) What is meant by saying it must be to the point? (5) It must be purposeful and systematic. (6) It must be complete. Inner characteristics of successful presentation are three: (1) Mental activity must be aroused. (2) This interest must be sustained, (3) and directed. Discuss these two classes of characteristics.

LESSON VIII.

(Comparison—Third Formal Step.)

1. Illustrate what is meant by this process. (1) Show how it works in and through the three stages of conception, judgment, and reason. Give illustration showing how comparison works in each of these stages. (2) Fixed standards of comparisons as to importance in classification; (3) as to value; (4) accuracy and clearness of thought. Show how standards of comparison are used in the various branches of study and phases of life.

2. *Association.*—How does association differ from comparison? (1) Give, illustrate, and explain the laws of association, (2) Discuss the practical application of these laws.

LESSON IX.

(Generalization and Application—Fourth and Fifth Steps.)

1. *Generalization.*—(1) Show that this is the highest stage of thinking. (2) Generalization as to form and order. In what grades should generalization be learned? Discuss, (1) "ideas before words." (2) Oral instruction (3) "Percepts before concepts." What is meant by the pedagogical paradox? What two errors does the author warn the teacher against?

2. *Application.*—(1) Knowledge gives culture. (2) Appied knowledge gives character. (3) Instruction that involves doing. (4) Experimentation. (5) Illustration. (6) Touching the interest of the community. Why is this step said to be the goal of instruction?

LESSON X.

(Thinking.)

Discuss thinking from the following topics:

1.   Importance of thinking.

2.   Exercises of the school not conducive to thinking.

3.   Observation employed so much in the school involves thinking.

4.   Demand the best effort by the pupil by avoiding two extremes. (1)   It is a mistake to give no help at all. (2)   It is a mistake to give too much help. Challenge the pupil's best effort, but do not discourage.

5.   Planful teaching which is separated into tests, instruction, assignment, stimulates thought. What form of drills make for thinking?

6.   Adapt your work to the stages of thinking—apprehension, comprehension.

7.   Two kinds of teachers—the mechanical and the spiritual, the artisan and the artist. Describe the experimental teacher. The teacher that is too ready to try suggestions. The teacher that teaches as he was taught. Planning for work—this is preparation.

8.   Emphasize observation and reflection as sources of knowledge. First and second hand information distinguished and considered as means. What is the Socratic method? Discuss these terms, applying them to the recitations: Examine, compare, discover, conclude, state, verify, etc.

LESSON XI.

(General Methods.)

1.   *General Methods Defined.*—A method is a systematic way of presenting the subject matter of knowledge in conformity to the laws of acquisition, reflection, and application of knowledge. General Methods deal with those fundamental characteristics that are common to all methods of whatsoever

kind. The five formal steps of teaching as discussed in the previous lessons constitute the typical form of the general method. The forms that follow simply emphasize different phases of it. Show how the laws of acquisition, reflection and application apply in this connection. Discuss the subject of method (1) as to theory, (2) as to practice.

2. *Analytic and Synthetic Methods.*—(1) Define and illustrate the terms analysis and synthesis. (2) Compare the use of these terms to those used in the typical form of the general method. (3) Discuss at length the analytic and synthetic order, in presenting the subject matter of geography, primary reading, spelling, etc.

3. *Inductive and Deductive Methods.*—(1) Define and fully illustrate the deductive and inductive modes of thought. (2) Show how these processes apply to the typical form of the general method. (3) In inductive-deductive teaching which process precedes the other? (4) What portion of the subject matter lends itself most easily to this phase of general method? Can one teach history or geography by this method?

(4) *Objective and Subjective Methods.*—(1) Explain the use of these terms: (2) What relation is sustained to the steps in the typical form? (3) Show that the so-called empirical and rational methods are simply other terms for the objective and subjective.

LESSON XII.

(Special and Individual Methods.)

1. *Special and Individual Methods Distinguished.*—Methods of teaching have characteristic differences as well as likenesses. These arise from the (1) nature of the subject matter involved, (2) and the means and devices used by the teacher in presenting it. The first has been denominated as "special methods," the second as "individual methods." In making this distinction it is not intended that any one particular method is the one designated to the exclusion of the other. But the same methods may be regarded from different points of view.

(2) *Special Methods.*—There are special methods in spelling, geography, language, arithmetic, etc. Illustrate. What are the different methods of teaching a child to read? Show that

three methods of approach are possible in presenting percentage, interest, or cubic root.

3. *Individual Methods.*—There are a great variety of individual methods depending upon the ingenuity of teachers. Individual methods are often limited in their use to a single lesson. Then there are others which serve as a convenient formula for presenting many lessons in the same or different subjects. A few of them are of so much importance that they deserve separate and detailed treatment.

4. *Lecture Method.*—(1) In its various forms what is it? (2) Its advantage and disadvantages to the teacher. (3) Discuss its advantages and disadvantages to the pupil. (4) With what grades is it best suited? What portion of the subject matter lends itself most readily to this method?

5. *The Topic Method.*—(1) Explain its nature. (2) Discuss its three forms—the verbal, the thought, the discussion. (3) Point out its merits and demerits. (4) Discuss carefully how to lead a child to recite by topics.

6. *Question and Answer Method.*—(1) The method explained. (2) Discuss questions as to form, guessing, content, developing, logical, direct and indirect, testing, leading and etc. (3) The advantage and the disadvantage of this method. (4) How would you use the printed question? (5) Discuss the Socratic method of questioning. (6) In actual practice how do these methods aid and supplement each other?

LESSON XIII.

(The Form of the Recitation.)

1. The oral work. (1) Indivdual methods how adapted to this form? (2) The advantages of the oral over the written. (3) Its adaptability to the various grades.

2. Written work. (1) advantages, (2) written preparation of lessons—advantages for busy work, of copying—(3) special recitations, note books, etc. (4) written recitations, (5) modes of correcting written work, (6) value arising from written exercises.

LESSON XIV.

(Recitation Tactics.)

1. Why are class tactics a necessity?

2. Discuss school tactics, class tactics, recitation tactics.

3. Justify or condemn the various methods of calling for answers.

4. Explain the form and determine the relative values of directing questions to the class.

LESSON XV.

(Text Books.)

1. The Adopted Texts of the Territory. When and how made? What are they? Object of uniformity. Is the adoption binding on all schools and all teachers?

2. Function of a text-book—treatise, monograph.

3. Characteristics of a good text in reading. arithmetic, geography, language, grammar, etc.

4. The intelligent use of a text presupposes that the teacher is qualified to furnish the proper approach. Discuss this topic thoroughly, especially as applicable to the lower grades.

5. Use of the texts in the various subjects. Should the subject matter of the texts be presented in the order indicated by the author? How should the oral and written exercises be related to each other, in arithmetic, for instance?

6. Discuss the question of supplementing the text.

Elementary Teaching and School Management

(This outline is based on "Teaching a District School" by Dinsmore, but teachers should consult "The Recitation" by Hamilton, "The Art of Teaching," by White, "The Educative Process" by Bagley, "Civics and Health" by Allen and "School Management" by White.)

LESSON I.

(Getting Ready to Teach.)

Study thoroughly the questions that a young teacher should ask herself, before commencing to teach: (1) Is my personal character adapted to the work? (2) Have my habits of life been such that my character, which is a resultant of same, will influence for good those with whom I come in contact? (4) What has been the character of my companionship during the formative period of my life? (5) Do I have positive convictions upon all questions of right or wrong? (6) What are the motives that prompt me in the desire for teaching? (7) Do I feel that I have some ability along the line of teaching? (8) Have I a good temper, one that will pilot me safely when annoying things take place in the school room? (9) Do I love all children with whom I come in contact in daily life? (10) Do I understand that teaching is not easy work, but on the contrary, rather strenuous labor?

(Steps in Preparation.)

(1.) What should be my general education before attempting to teach? (2) Why is special and professional training necessary for a young teacher? (3) Is reading of books and papers along literary and professional lines, a habit; and if so, is it important that a young teacher get this habit early in her teaching career? (4) By observation, what is it possible for a young teacher to learn, that may benefit her, when she goes into the school room? (5) What are the legal requirements for first, second and third grade certificates in New Mexico? (6) How may a young teacher prepare to take the third grade certificate examination, or the "Reading Circle" examination?

SECURING A SCHOOL.

(1) Why should a young teacher be very careful in selecting her first work? (2) What is the best form of application, and how should it be presented? (3) Of what benefit is a contract with school officers, and what stipulations should be in the contract to protect the teacher and the school district?

BEFORE SCHOOL OPENS.

(1) What preliminary work should a teacher do before the first day of school? (2) How may a young teacher get the co-operation of parents and pupils early in her school work?

FIRST DAY OF SCHOOL.

Prepare a program and present same before the class for the criticism of class and instructor.

Let the program be for a district school with the following conditions:

There are thirty-five pupils in the school in grades as follows:
First grade—9 pupils.
Second grade—7 pupils.
Third grade—6 pupils.
Fourth grade—6 pupils.
Fifth grade—4 pupils.
Sixth grade—3 pupils.

At the close of discussion the instructor to present a model program for a district school with above conditions.

LESSON II.

(1) Discuss the fundamental purpose of the school.

(2) What is the real function of the teacher?

(3) Is it important that the young teachers understand thoroughly, parental duties, parental rights and responsibilities?

(4) Is it quite as important that pupils and patrons have a mutual understanding as to the duties, rights and responsibilities of the teacher?

(5) Duties of school officers.

(6) What is the necessity of the teacher being on the most intimate and confidential terms with her school officers and county school superintendent?

(7). What school reports are required by law or by direction of the Territorial Superintendent, under statutory provisions?

(8) Why are reports important?

(9) Upon what basis should pupils be classified in the school room, and what reports (of previous terms) help the teacher in making the classification?

(10) What general rules of school should be adopted at the beginning of school work, and why should promptness and regularity be strictly enforced?

(11) What general and specific rules of conduct should be given and of what importance upon the school is the teacher's conduct?

(12) What should be the character of "Opening Exercises?"

(13) Discuss the model program presented by the instructor in Lesson I.

(14) What are the points of excellence in any program?

Lesson III.

(1) The importance of the correct assignment of a lesson in the various grades and classes. When and how an assignment should be made. Character of an efficient assignment. What must a teacher know as regards the ability of the class, the character of the text or subject to be studied? How, and with what care should lessons in language, reading, geography and numbers be assigned?

(2) What is the importance of "Busy Work" in keeping the lower grades orderly during the time, when they are not in class, and what should be the character of this work?

Discuss the vital features of the lesson-period from the following points; enables pupils to tell when they have learned; it enables the teacher to correct faulty notions that may have been acquired by the individual study of the pupil; it shows whether or not the pupil comprehends the lesson or the subject matter presented; it gives the child confidence in the matter of expressing himself in good English; it enables the teacher to vitalize the subject matter presented and to correlate it with the practical affairs of life; it enables the teacher, to test, to teach and to train.

(3)   What is meant by teaching:
If good results come from teaching, what must have been the activities of the teacher and pupil to bring about the results? In what manner does simple plain language on part of teacher, bring about good results in teaching? Why are good illustrations of such great importance in clinching concepts of things learned?

(4)   Is there an art of questioning? Discuss the proper manner of presenting questions so that the pupils' knowledge may be drawn upon, and his activities brought into action, whenever a subject is presented for contemplation. What is meant by the Socratic method of questioning?

(5)   Why are reviews necessary and discuss the relative importance of oral and written reviews.

(6) What is attention? What are the factors of attention? What are the most important laws of attention? What is the key of attention? Why is attention so important?

(7)   What is meant by interest? When does a child acquire an inerest in anything, and when may he *lose* his interest in that thing? What part does the teacher play in causing children to take an interest in studies, and is she ever responsible for pupils *losing* interest in certain studies?

(8)   What is meant by character building, and what of its importance? Has character a physical basis? Discuss the effect of good manners and good morals upon child life in the school room. Can the teacher influence her pupils for good, by exemplifying, in her daily life and conduct the most excellent principles of spiritual, moral, physical and intellectual life?

(9)   What is meant by good order in the school room? Is a school a well ordered republic? Is obedience to lawful authority necessary? Do the cardinal principles of industry, honesty, sobriety, tend to develop good citizenship? Are the common sources of disorder in the school room, natural or unnatural conditions? Are they the outgrowth of misdirected energies? Is the teacher largely responsible for disorder?

(10)   Discuss the educational value of rest periods, and the teacher's influence in directing these periods, so that the pupils may get the most out of them. What physical games or exercises may be permitted during recesses and noons, that may

redound to the best interests of all concerned? In what way should the teacher identify herself with these games or sports?

LESSON IV.

(1)   What is meant by the "Compulsory School Law" in New Mexico? Whose duty is it to enforce it? Who are exempt from attendance under this law? What is the punishment of parents or guardians who are convicted for not obeying this law? Does public sentiment justify the rigorous enforcement of this law?

(2)   What effect does chronic absence of a pupil have upon his progress through school? What effect does absenteeism have upon the school in general? How may a teacher reduce her cases of absence to a minimum? Can parents be made to see that they have a moral obligation in the matter of seeing to it that their children are regular and punctual in all matters? Has the teacher a moral obligation to perform in looking after those who are irregular in attendance?

(3)   What are the main causes and what are the evil effects of tardiness? What is the best plan towards remedying this evil? What effect will the personal habits of the teacher have upon the conduct of pupils in the matter of punctuality?

(4)   If it is true, that the school building, with its surroundings, represent the average culture of a community, it it necessary that this building have the proper attention that it may be kept in the very best condition? Should the building site be healthful and beautiful? Should the building be properly heated, lighted and ventilated? Should proper sanitary conditions prevail throughout the building and grounds?

(5)   Why is there a necessity for general "good will among the pupils of a school? In what way may a teacher adjust causes of ill-will, that may arise at times?

(6)   Why is sanitation so important to the health of the school? Has a teacher a moral obligation in seeing to it that healthful conditions prevail? Is disease the result of the violation of the laws of health? What is a contagious disease? How are contagious diseases gotten? What are the statutory provisions towards preventing the spread of contagious disease?

(7) Discuss the several "Laws of Health," and is good health a civic obligation?

(8) What are the "Seven Health Motives and Seven Catch Words" discussed by Dr. Allen in "Civics and Health", (Reading Circle Book)?

(9) Why are "Physical Exercises of great benefit in a school?

(10) What is the value of "Rhetorical Exercises," in a school? Should the teacher censor all productions that are to be given?

Lesson V.

(1) What should be the true spirit of the teacher? What prompts the teacher to greater endeavor?

(2) What should be a teacher's attitude towards the best or worst conditions of school?

(3) How, and by whom may a teacher be encouraged, and how and when may she encourage those who are under her immediate direction?

(4) How may a teacher get a thorough knowledge of the branches she will be expected to teach? How may she get a theoretical knowledge of the proper methods of teaching subjects and of disciplining children? How may she get a practical knowledge of the same?

(5) Can a professional spirit be improved by one's daily reading of literature, professional and otherwise, by visiting good schools, by attending teachers' meetings or associations?

(6) What devices may a teacher use in order to keep up an interest in work? What days may be celebrated that will enable the teacher to develop an historical interest, or some other interest that will be helpful to the school?

(7) Is it well to have "School Visitors" occasionally?

Lesson VI.

(1) What is meant by "heart power," in the matter of controlling pupils   It is said that the great Swiss reformer Pestalozzi controlled by means of love. What was his success? How is the teacher in the school room to show her love for all pupils, either good or bad? How may a teacher show a boy whom she feels compelled to punish, that she loves him?

(2) How do children manifest their love for parents and teachers, or for one another? When a child in the school room, feels an enmity towards these parties, what effect will these have upon his material progress or his general conduct?

(3) Do children of different degrees of goodness or badness, brightness or dullness need special or individual treatment?

(4) Do children with defective eyes or ears need special attention and care?

(5) It is said that the best index to community health is the physical condition of school children. If true, what is the teacher's moral duty in the matter?

Lesson VII.

(1) Why do some people today say that the work of the school is not practical? Is there an effort on the part of school people to meet this criticism, and to make the schools of today meet the twentieth century requirements? Has there been an effort on the part of teachers to improve Reading in our schools? Do school libraries increase the desire for good reading? Are children encouraged to read in their homes?

(2) What effort is being made by elementary school teachers to encourage an acquisition of good English on the part of school children, and why are the results obtained, not commensurate with the efforts put forth by teachers? Do teachers correct all errors of language, both oral and written, and insist at all times in oral language, the proper word, its correct pronunciation and accentuation, and in written language, the proper form and meaning of word, its correct spelling, capitalization, etc? Do teachers insist that pupils use the dictionary to learn correct spelling and diacritical markings and shades of meanings of words? Critics say that we do not insist on these matters as vigorously as we ought to do. Is the criticism just?

(3) Is the teaching of Geography done in our schools, so as to make it practical? Is the teaching of this branch so correlated with industrial and commercial progress, that the child is enabled to see the benefit that will accrue from its study? Is the use of the map or globe so taught that this apparatus has a symbolic meaning to the child and imaginative conceptions are formed in children's minds, of places and things they have never

seen? Are teachers correlating geography and history in such
a way as to create a greater interest in both of these branches?
How may these be correlated?

(4)   Why are biography and folk lore tales the beginning
of Elementary History?

Do little children love to admire the character of great and
good men, by merely hearing some one read about them?
Will these same children, when they grow older, select more
extended works, descriptive of the men or women they learned
to love in their now youthful days? Do the books that a child
reads in his youth, influence his character?

(5)   Can the true function of our government be taught to
children by the use of proper juvenile literature in the homes
and schools?

Lesson VIII.

(1)   Why is arithemtic considered such a difficult study
for teachers or pupils, when they come to take examinations?
Is it because it is not properly taught in the elementary
schools? Why are many schools introducing mental arithmetic
into their grades? Many topics that were in arithmetics twenty
years ago are now eliminated.   Does it improve arithmetic as
a study to have these matters dropped?   Are boys and girls
being taught to reason quickly and accurately by the modern
teaching?

(2)   Why should teachers study hygiene and physiology?
Is it necessary that the teacher know the laws of growth of
the human system? Should she know what foods nourish or
build up the system, or what material tears down the same?
Should she know what exercises strengthen and develop the
physical and intellectual powers and what activities destroy the
same? Is it important that the teacher undersand the relation
of animals and plants?

(3)   Why is the great business world lending its influence
in favor of temperance? Why are young men who are sober
and industrious in such demand today?·

(4)   Many schools are now adding commercial departments
to their work.   Penmanship, spelling, letter writing, business
forms commercial arithmetic, commercial geography, commercial law, typewriting and stenography are some of the subjects

taught. Why should there be such a demand for these branches to be specially taught?

Lesson IX.

(1) What are some of the chief industries of New Mexico? Is it well for a teacher in a community where some particular industry is prevalent, to interest herself in that special industry and show its relation to other industries of the world? A teacher in the New Mexico schools should be able to locate all mining centers, whether coal, copper or other minerals, and to locate manufacturing, commercial and agricultural (Farming or Stock Raising) centers. Can you do so? Does it argue that if a farmer has been a success at crop raising, stock raising or fruit raising in any one of the following states: Kansas, Missouri, Indiana, Illinois, Oklahoma or Texas, he would succeed in a similar way in New Mexico? What are some of the problems that he would be compelled to learn should he come to New Mexico?

(2) Why has farming in the past few years taken on a scientific aspect? Several states of the union now make the elements of agriculture one of the studies to be taught in the public schools? Why has there been a demand for this branch of elementary science? Do we any longer think that any one can manage a farm successfully in any way he might choose? Why was there a commission appointed to investigate the cause why so many leave the farm? Many able writers and thinkers are now attempting to stop the tide that now flows from rural life to city life, by showing up the evils of congested cities, and presenting the many advantages of country life in comparison. Are they justified in so doing?

(3) Where is the Agricultural College of New Mexico, and what effort is it putting forth to help farming, fruit raising and stock raising in the territory? What bulletins may be secured from this institution that would be of great assistance in an agricultural industry in the territory?

(4) School gardens are maintained in some communities. What is it possible for a child to learn from these? Why is there a growing demand in several of the larger cities of our territory for manual training and domestic science in the high schools and grades? In several of the Eastern states these

things are now being taught Can we reasonably expect that they will come to us in time?

(4) What professions are taught in the state schools at Albuquerque, Las Vegas, Silver City, Socorro, Las Cruces.

LESSON X.

(1) In what way does personal magnetism, natural aptitude and special preparation, assist one in the elements of governing? Of what importance is a strong and well cultivated will? What moral code ought a teacher to adopt, if he proposes to get the good will of pupils and people generally?

(2) When order means system, how may this be acquired in a school room? When order means the good behavior of pupils, how may this be acquired? Why should order and system prevail in all public schools?

(3) What is punishment and when is it thought best to administer the same? Are there proper and improper modes of punishment?

(3) What is the specific aim of the public school? Are our schools today disseminating a general knowledge that is of use to mankind? Are the schools instrumental in developing the minds of boys and girls? Are habits being formed that will enable boys and girls to think clearly and reason logically on all the affairs of citizen life? In short, is good character being formed? Discuss the above points.

(4) What is the relation of habit to training? Why are *right* habits so essential? How may a teacher train boys and girls in the formation of good habits?

Orthography

LESSON I.

1. *Reform Spelling.*—Give the argument for and against simplified spelling. What words are included in the list?
2. Discuss and fully illustrate the advantages of grouping words for spelling—according (1) to the number of syllables, (2) to homonyms, (3) to sound and rythm, (4) to derivation, (5) to the difficulty in spelling, (6) to synonyms, (7) to occupations, parts of objects, sciences, etc., (8) to false orthography, (9) to filling of blanks calling for choice of meaning.
3. Give the argument for and against the use of the spelling text in school.
4. Give the author's (Reed) reason for making this text.
5. Why are some pupils better spellers than others?

LESSON II.

1. Learn, recite and fully illustrate all the rules for spelling in the text. Of what value are they?
2. Give and illustrate the use of capital letters.
3. Point out the means used by the dictionary to teach proper pronunciation .Why should you teach syllabication?
4. Show how phonograms are used in teaching spelling and reading.

LESSON III.

1. Classify the elements of speech into tonics, subtonics and atonics.
2. What are the terms applied by the text for these classes of elements?
3. Point out the cognates of the language.
4. Show the position of the organs of speech in making these—in both initial and terminal positions.

Lesson IV.

1. Illustrate the Webster diacritical markings for all the vowels and consonants, committing an illustrative word for each.

2. Make a table of the elementary sounds of the language and bring to the class.

Lesson V.

Select a list of words from the text of most difficult pronunciation and conduct a pronouncing contest thereon.

Lesson VI.

There are three senses concerned in learning to spell: sight, hearing and muscle. The images of sight and hearing in some instances may conflict with each other, but usually these three senses reinforce one another in association. Hence, the value of oral, phonic, written and sight spelling.

1. The preparation—(1) Co-operation of teacher and pupils.—The teacher drills pupils on the pronunciation of the words by marking the accent, by marking the vowels in the accented syllable, and by striking out the silent letters. The meaning is taught by analysis, definition, and use. (Never mark any other vowel except the one in the accented syllable. If you do, there is confusion. Even the dictionary does not attempt it.) (2) Independent effort of the pupil Teach the child to, first, form an eye-image of the word; second, hold it in his mind in a reflective way; third, reproduce it in writing; fourth, carefully repeat the process; fifth, use the word in a sentence.

2. Recitation.—The recitation may occur in either of two forms—written or oral. Discuss and determine the value of the various devices you have used in connection with these two methods. Have the child write the words as a whole.

3. Conduct an exercise illustrative of the above plan.

Lessons VII. VIII, IX, X.

1. Give the etymological definition of the following words: Benediction, circumnavigate, talking, blamable acquitted, spinner, reddest, gladden, tardiness, protestant, inspect, abstract, consciousness, transportation, influence, animation, un-

derrate, inflexible, repugnant, valedictory, manufactory, composition.

2. Give an illustrative lesson in synonyms from the text, another on choice of words, another on misused words. When would you begin to teach the child to spell by writing? Would you teach him to print? In what grade of work should oral spelling begin. If a word is written incorrectly, why is it advisable to erase it without calling attention to the mistake? In what stage of advancement can mistakes in form be freely discussed with profit? In oral spelling would you pass a word from one pupil, giving each a chance to guess? Why not? Do you believe in head marks? Why? Would you allow pupils to correct each other's mistakes in written spelling? Why? In reviews is it not waste of time to assign the easy as well as the difficult words for study and recitation? It is said that formal definitions should not be taught before the fourth grade. In what other ways may the meaning of words be taught? A primary idea is its own definition. A secondary idea is one that is defined by pointing out its relation to other ideas. How would you teach the meaning of these primary or unclassifiable words as to meaning?

Discuss the question of spelling in connection with the reading. Does oral spelling assist the reading? Does the reading assist the spelling? What per cent. of the words of the reader should the child be able to spell as a qualification for promotion? Would you teach a child to spell a word he could not define? Discuss the teaching of the use of the dictionary as to time, method, etc. Illustrate the correct manner of writing words and their definitions. The use of a language implies four arts: (1) the interpretation of spoken words, (2) to utter them, (3) to interpret the written form, (4) to write the form.

What have these to do with spelling? Why is English spelling difficult? Would you make every lesson a spelling lesson? What is meant by the dictionary habit in this connection? There are two hundred thousand or more words in the dictionary. What words among these should one learn to spell? Why is a misspelled word considered a disgrace among people of culture? Does a child's word memory assist him in learning spelling? How would you hold pupils responsible for remembering the words which have been taught them?

Assign one of these problems to members of the Institute and have a report given the next day.

1. What words should make up the spelling list? Number of words for a lesson?

2. How to interest pupils in spelling.

3. The relative amount of oral and written spelling.

4. The pronouncing of words.

5. Correction of papers.

6. How to prevent deception.

7. How to assist pupils who endeavor to learn, but who constantly miss words.

8. Would you deduct for misspelled words in other lessons?

9. How would you appeal to the reasoning activity of the child in learning to spell?

10. The use of the dictionary.

Penmanship

(The following outline is arranged with a view to improving the writing of teachers, thereby suggesting methods of improving their writing classes. The Manual of Medial Writing, Ginn & Co., should be in the hands of every teacher. Let the Instructor assign a definite amount of the following outline for each lesson):

1. Discuss—(1) Importance of good copies; (2) The best method of writing: (3) Why should the lesson be short?; (4) Time to have the writing exercise; (5) The pride of pupil and teacher as shown in accuracy and neatness of work; (6) Writing to ruled lines; (7) Importance of having the initial effort correct.

2. Material required.—(1.) Ink, (2) pens, (3) penholders. Describe the position of the book, the hand, the body. As these are described, illustrate them.

3. Show how waking-up exercises on the cover page are to be used. Let these steps be followed: (1) Instruct, (2) illustrate, (3) retrace the copy with dry pen, (4) practice the copy in ink.

4. Give the author's rules for writing on the black-board. (1) Position, (2) follow your arm, (3) write on a level with the eye, (4) holding the crayon, (5) using it.

5. Make an illustrative chart showing the spacing of all letters and figures. Take up each specimen and discuss it as to (1) form, (2) slant, (3) spacing, (4) method of making.

6. Group the letters according to their similarity of form, and the difficulty of their making.

7. Plan of the books.—(1) Utilizing space. (2) Size and shape of the books. (3) The advanced and review work. (4) Sentiment expressed by the copy. (5) Dealing with absentees. (6) Grading of the books. (7) Legibility. (8) Steadiness of improvement. (9) Uniformity. (10) Size.

8. Discuss devices for securing the best results in conducting the writing class.

Psychology

"A Primer of Psychology" by Pitchner, published by the MacMillan Company, Chicago, will serve as a suitable text for this course.

Lesson I.

(Introductory.)

1. Give the derivative meaning of the word, psychology. Psychology is a *science* which *observes* and *explains mental states* and processes. Discuss the italicised words in this definition. Distinguish things from processes, the objective from the subjective point of view. From whence comes the facts of psychology? How do you know that other people have minds? Discuss the methods of psychology. What are the difficulties connected with each?

Lesson II.

(Mind and Consciousness in General.)
1. Consciousness defined.
2. Consciousness distinguished from mind.
3. Character of consciousness, (1) Self-consciousness, (2) Content or quality, (3) Continuity, (4) Intensity or rise and fall of consciousness, (5) Speed or time rate of consciousness.
4. Divisions of mind, (1) Mind has three stages. Child—adult—old age. Briefly compare them. (2) Conscious states, what are they? (3) What is meant by concrete processes? (4) Elementary processes defined and illustrated.
5. What are some of the problems of psychology?

LESSON III.

(Mind and Body.)

1. What is the mind? What is the body?

2. Give the evidences that the brain is the organ of consciousness. What are the functions of the various portions of the nervous system? Distinguish afferent from efferent nerves.

3. Give the general effects of, mind upon body, body upon mind.

4. Distinguish movement from action. Explain and illustrate reflex movement, automatic movement.

5. Describe the organs of the special senses.

6. For every psychological process there is a corresponding physiological process. What is meant by psychophysical parallelism? Show that mind is not a function of the brain. What is the physiological condition of consciousness? Attention? Habit? Temperament? Memory? Association, etc?

LESSON IV.

(Sensations.)

1. Light waves produce a chemical change on the retina of the eye. This stimulus starts in the optic nerve a commotion or current, which is carried to the optic center of the brain, there to be elaborated—a *physiological process*. On the mind side as result of this, consciousness has a sensation of light and color —a *conscious process*.

In like manner show how all the sensations are produced. From these illustrations it may be seen that there are three classes of elements concerned in sensation.

2. Elements of Physical Environment.—Not only point out the nature of the stimulus for each organ of sense, but how it affects the organ.

3. The physiological elements involve: (1) An end organ capable of converting a physical energy into a physiological energy. (2) Nerve tracts capable of transmitting nerve energy from the end organ of the brain. (3) A brain capable of adjusting itself to all the incoming currents of the organism.

4. The Psychic Elements: (1) It is necessary for the mind to respond to the sensory condition of the brain. (2) The mind is changed or modified thereby. (3) This modification is the stuff out of which a knowledge of the outer world is made.

5. Bear in mind the following facts: (1) Sensations are complex affairs. Show that there can be no such thing as a single sensation. (2) We are not aware of sensations at all, we simply experience a knowledge of things. (3) Sensations are psychic affairs and they are classified according to the different sense organs.

6. Kinds of sensation. Show that the specific character of sensations depends upon, (1) the character of the particular sense organ, (2) The portions of the organ stimulated, (3) The variation in the kind of stimuli, (4) The length of time the stimulus acts, (5) The intensity of the stimulus. Make an outline of the various sensations on the basis suggested.

7. Define a sensation.

8. Discuss the education of the senses, (1) as to extent, (2) as to its influence on the entire mind.

LESSON V.

(Perception.)

1. Define perception. What is its relation to sensation? Point out the differences between perceptions and ideas. What then are the various concrete and elementary processes involved in a perception?

2. Discuss the classes of perceptions, (1) as to quality, space and time. (2) As to senses involved, eye, ear, etc.

3. Show the illusory elements in all perception. What is meant by hallucinations.

4. Discuss these principles: (1) The senses through perception are capable of a high degree of development. (2) By educating the senses we educate the whole mind. (3) A knowledge of the world is based upon different data from a knowledge of the mind. (4) The process of unifying sensation, making them meaningful is called apperception. Its basis is laid in the nervous system and is expressed by "acquired and inherited tendencies."

LESSON VI.

(Ideation.)

1. An idea is a copy or a reproduction of a past experience, a memory image. Explain the meaning of idea from its etymology. Show how ideas are obtained.

2.   Ideas compared with perception. We cannot perceive without ideas but ideas originate in perception. There are three particulars in which ideas differ from their original experiences, (1) Intensity, (2) Completeness of detail or content. (3) Objectivity—they may or may not be referred to some particular objective experience.

4.   Law of association.—Ideas or perceptions occurring together in an original experience tend to persist. In reproduction the same connection or order adheres. Association is thus explained by the law of habit. Show that ideas only are associated. Give the formula for association.

5.   Forms of associations. (1) stimultaneous, (2) successive.   Illustrate each of these.

6.   Conditions favorable for associations. (1) Similarity and contrast. (2) Cause and effect. (3) Continuty of time and space. (4) Means and ends, etc.

7.   How do ideas become abstract or general?

Lesson VII.

(Feelings, Emotions and Sentiments.)

1.   Two theories of feeling. One theory regards feeling as primary, unanalizable, and standing as its own definition. Its very essence is in the being felt. The other theory regards it as a concrete process. Affective consciousness—pleasantness and unpleasantness is primary. Feeling is a complex process made up of sensations and affections. When the asseptive side receives the emphass one says he feels so and so.

2.   Feelings are subjective while sensations as such are objective. Illustrate. How do sensations differ from feeling?

3.   Discuss feelings as to kind.

4.   Discuss emotions after this outline. (1) Feeling, emotions, mood, passions and sentiments, distinguished. (2) Trace the course of an emotion. (3) How are emotions classified. (5) *Discuss temperament* as to (1) definition, (2) Kinds, etc.

6.   Sentiments distinguished from emotion .

7.   The various forms of sentiments distinguished.

8.   Intellectual sentiments. (1) Definition, (2) Belief, (3) Truth, (4) Curiosity.

9.   Social or ethical sentiments. (1) Defined, (2) Kinds.

10.   Aesthetic sentiments. (1) Definition, (2) Kinds.

Lesson VIII.

(Memory and Imagination.)

1. What is meant by a memory? An imagination? How do these processes differ? How are they alike?

2. Active and passive forms distinguished.

3. Stages of memory—retention, reproduction and recognition.

4. Discuss the art of committing, art of remembering, art of forgetting.

5. Dangers and uses of the imagination.

6. Kinds of memory and of imagination, distinguished. What are the bases of this classification?

7. Limitations of the imagination.

Lesson IX.

(Thought and Langauge.)

1. Any set of movements common to a group of individuals mutually recognizable as a sign of a mental process is called language. In your analysis of this definition note the following: (1) All mental processes have a tendency to express themselves. (2) Language is a mutual means of exchanging emotions, ideas and thoughts, (3) There is no other means of expressing a mental state except through the use of the motor organism. (4) The developing of thought and language must proceed together. (5) The function of mental suggestion—positive and adverse. (6) Imitation as a motive for language.

2. There are two kinds of language, (1) gesture, which is subjective and used to express the emotional side, and (2) articulate speech which is objective, which is used to express the thought side. How do these two kinds stand related as to development? What were the first forms of language and speech?

3. Discuss words as (.1) movable types, (2) as a support and stimulus to thought.

4. What is thinking? It is a mental movement from one idea or relation to another, with a clear consciousness of the relations. Show how the process varies from very simple forms to those of more elaborate character. Discuss judgment, concept, reason, comparison, abstraction, generalization, etc. Define and illustrate the inductive form of reasoning, deductive

forms. Does a child reason? An animal? Give incidents. Show
that reasoning de novo is a rare process.

LESSON X.

(Will, Attention, Action.)

1. A developed form of will is a selective action that knows
what it wants. In a well defined act of choice or resolve, there
are several stages: (1) Two or more possible *lines* of possible
action are recognized. (2) an excitement of a *desire* as to the
value of these different courses of procedure. (3) *Deliberating*
upon the consequences of actions. (4) The *decision* cuts off the
deliberation. (5) The consciousness of *doing* something. Illustrate these steps. Upon what does the development of the will
depend? What is the primary element in every form of will?

2. Discuss attention as a form of will. Attention is a primary form of all mental processes. What is meant by inatten-
tion? The rise and fall of attention. The distribution of attention. Active, passive and secondary passive attention distinguished. Importance of training the attention in education.

3. Explain carefully the simple forms of doing, such as im-
pulsive, reflex, automatic, instinctive. Which are actions?
Which are movements?

Physics

In the discussion of the following lessons, first consider the topic. What it is, how does it work, and lastly of what practical value is it to civilization?

Lesson I.

The historic standard of length, origin of the metric system. The fundamental units. Definition of destiny. Resolution of forces. Law of gravitation. Equilibrium. Velocity. Acceleration. Momentum. Centrifugal force.

Lesson II.

Liquid pressure beneath a free surface. The hydrostatic paradox. The hydraulic press. The hydraulic elevator. Artesian wells. Specific gravity. Hydrometer. Torriceli's experiment. Barometer. Incompressibility of liquids. Compressibility of air. Density of air below sea level. Siphon; air pump. The Cartesian diver. The diving bell.

Lesson III.

Diffusion of gases and liquids. Saturated vapor. Pressure of a saturated vapor. Dew. Fog. Rain. Hail, Snow. Humidity. Evaporation. Hydrometer. Sublimation. Elasticity. Cohesion. Capillary action. Crystalization. Absorption.

Lesson IV.

Kinds of thermometers. Change from one reading to another. How grade a thermometer? Maximum and minimum thermometers. Coefficient of expansion. Compensating pendulum. Erg. Fixed pulley. Movable pulleys. Combinations of pulleys. Levers. Wheel and axle. The screw. Horse power. Potential and kinetic energy.

Lesson V.

Friction. Ball bearing. Internal friction. Water turbine. A calorie. The conservation of energy. Perpetual motion. Condensing and non-condensing engines. The eccentric. The governor. Efficiency of steam. Mechanism of the gas engine. The steam turbine.

Lesson VI.

Heat of fusion. Latent heat. Regelation. Heat of vaporization. Variation of the boiling point with pressure. Cooling by solution. Freezing mixture. Fractional distillation. The liquid air machine. Manufactured ice. Cold storage. Conduction. Connection and radiation of heat. The Davy Safety lamp. Ventilation.

Lesson VII.

Magnets, magnetic fields. Dip of the compass needle. Magnetic pole. Kinds of electrification. Conductors. Electron theory. Induction. Lighting. Electric screens. Condensers. Toepler-Holtz machine. Cell. Direction of current. Galvanometer. Ohm. Ampere. Shuts. Polarization. Cells arranged in series and parallel.

Lesson VIII.

The electrolysis of water. Electro-plating. Electro-typing, Refining of metals. Storage batteries. Helix. Electro magnet. Electric bell. Telegraph. Heating effects. Incandescent lamps. Arc lamps. The Cooper-Hewitt mercury lamp. Induced current. An alternating surrent dynamo. The multiplolar alternator. Commutator. The ring-armature direct current dynamo. Series, shunt, and compound-wound dynamos. Electric motor. Induction coil. Telephone.

Lesson IX.

Sources of sound. Speed of transmission. Speaking tubes. Longitudinal and transverse waves. The siren. Speaking gallery. Sounding boards. Beats. Interference. The major diatonic scale. Law of lengths and tensions. Manometric flames. Overtures. The phonograph. How did Roemer discover the speed of light? Eclipses. Pholometer. Diffused light. Refraction. Polarization.

Lesson X.

Multiple images. Virtual image. Camera. The projecting lantern. Telescope. Zeiss binocular. Wave lengths of light of various colors. Newton's color disk. Color of pigments. Color of films. Chromatic aberration. The rain-bow. Infra red rays. Wireless telegraphy. Roentgen ray and its uses. The disintegration of radio-active substances. The birth of radium.

Part II
ELEMENTARY COURSES
FOR
Third Grade Applicants

ARITHMETIC

(The instructor will carefully inspect the following outline and divide it into twenty (20) lessons for the four weeks' institute, according to the needs of the class. Use adopted text.)

This course is designed primarily as exercises in review for teachers who should become more thorough in the subject of arithmetic. With this in view each lesson should be briefly presented by the Instructor before assigning it to members of the institute for study. Should an inductive initial presentation of any subject be desired, select topics from the various divisions to suit the end sought. One hour should be given to home study and its results submitted in some form to the Instructor. It is useless to attempt to cover the whole subject of even elementary arithmetic in so short a time, but be thorough in what is attempted and be sure to throw the emphasis upon those portions most needed.

(Notation and Numeration.)

1. Give meaning to these terms: Notation, numeration, integer, fraction; distinguish a common from a decimal fraction.

2. Name the first twelve periods and show the use of the comma, the period, and "and" in reading decimals.

3. Show the relation (1) of orders to each other, (2) of orders to periods, (3) the use of naught.

4. In 674.346 give (1) the local value of each figure, (2) the relative value of each to all the others. In the same manner, read $341.365. Read (6—1-2 plus 5x7)—13. See the adopted text for similar exercises.

5. Write (1) three hundred six billion one hunded nine; (2) three thousand sixty-one hundred millionths, both as a decimal, and as a common fraction; (3) five thousand four and twenty-one hundred thousandths.

6.   Make original rules for integer and decimal notation and
numeration.

ADDITION.

1.   Show that only numbers of the same kind can be add‑
ed. Illustrate this principle (1) By adding numbers consisting
of units, tens, hundreds, etc.; (2) By adding U. S. money;
(3) By adding compound denominate numbers; (4) By adding
fractions.

2.   Develop rules (1) for adding integers and decimals; (2)
for adding common fractions; (3) for adding compound de
nominate numbers. First let the directions apply to individual
exercises, then follow by expressing them in a most general
way.

3.   Solve and explain the following exercises, giving special
attention to the written and oral language forms, (1) 14.68
plus 6x95.04 plus 896.87; (2) 3-7 plus 11-20 plus 33-45; (3)
4 3-4 plus 23 5-9 plus 27 10-13 plus 45 4-5; (4) To 9 yards, 7
feet, 11 inches add 12 yards, 9 feet, 7 inches.

4.   Solve these problems found in the text and hand them
to the instructor for correction; Ex. 51, No. 10; Ex. 126,
Nos. 3, 6, 15, 18; P. 179; Ex. 357, Nos. 7, 8, 9, 10, (Walsh's
New Grammar School Arithmetic).

5.   The first year a man worked in a smelter he received
$460. If his salary is increased $75.00 a year for five years,
how much does he earn in six years?

6.   A man has gone 17 3-4 miles of his journey, which is
9 5-6 miles less than the distance he has yet to go. What is
the length of the journey?

7.   The adjacent sides of a rectangular field are respectively
40 rods, 10 feet, 8 inches, and 34 rods, 9 feet, 4 inches. What
is the distance around it?

8.   Explain these problems from the text without solving
them: P. 54, No. 16; P. 58, No. 10; P. 67, No. 14; P. 69, No.
14; P. 139, No. 21.

SUBTRACTION.

1.   Give meaning by illustration and by definition to the
following terms: Subtraction, minuend, subtrahend, remainder.

2.   Principles—show by concrete illustration that only like

num'ers can be subtracted; (2) The minuend is equal to the sum of the subtrahend and the remainder. How many objects are required to illustrate the process of subtraction?

3. Bring to class practical exercises illustrating the three problems in subtraction; (1) the minuend and the subtrahend given, to find remainder; (2) the remainder and the subtrahend given, to find the minuend (3) minuend and the remainder given, to find the subtrahend.

4. Explain these exercises—(1) 847—218; (2) 904—329; (3) 9—.0678; (4) 4 3-4x6 2-5—3.7; (5) From 10 lb. 10 pwt. 10 gr. take 5 lb. 11 oz. 12 pwt. 13 gr.; (6) From 7-8 A. take 31.5 sq. rds.

5. For drill exercise bring in the following: P. 28, Nos. 10, 20; P. 33, Nos. 2, 11; P. 66, Nos. 13, 22, 26, 29; P. 135, Nos. 3, 5, 7.

6. Deduce a rule for subtraction.

7. A man owes $3780, but has only $2860. How much must he borrow to pay the debt?

8. A boy bought a book for $2 3-10, a knife for $3-4, and a hat for $1 3-5. What change should he receive from a ten dollar bill?

8. How long since the Declaration of Independence? The death of Lincoln?

10. Write out the explanation of the following and bring to the class:—(1) P. 56, Nos. 27, 29, 33, 36; (2) P. 112, Nos. 8, 15, 17, 19, 22, 23, 36, 38; (3) P. 284, No. 3.

MULTIPLICATION.

1. Give meaning to the terms: ratio, multiplication, multiplier, multiplicand, product.

2. Principles:—(1) show that multiplication is a short method of addition; (2) that the multiplier is always abstract; (3) that the product is like the multiplicand; (4) that the product is numerically the same using either number as the multiplier.

3. Bring practical exercises to illustrate the three problems:—(1) the multiplier and the multiplicand given, to find the product; (2) the product and the multiplier given, to find the multiplicand; (3) the product and the multiplicand given, to find the multiplier.

4. Explain these exercises:—(1) 832x3; (2) 796x8; (3)

847x24; (4) 54.6x8.9; (5) 23-45x55-138; (6) 467x3-5; (7)
4 3-9x8 7-9; (8) 8.3x1 3-7; (9) 6 times 213 rods, 1 yard, 2
feet, 6 inches; (10) 3-4 of 25 gallons, 2 quarts, 1 pint, 2 gills.

5. Drill exercises from the text:—P. 29, Nos. 3, 4, 10;
P. 86, Nos. 7, 10, 16, 19; P. 106, Ex. 180, No. 8; Ex. 181,
No. 6; Ex. 182, No. 10; Ex. 183, No. 1.

6. At the rate of 2 sheep for $5, how many sheep can be
bought for 25 five dollar bills?

7. If 2 1-2 of an inch on a certain map represent a mile,
what is the distance on the map between two places that are
40 miles apart?

8. When vinegar is 3c a pint, how much is 7-8 of a gallon
worth?

9. Write out and hand in the analysis for the following:
P. 54, Nos. 7, 14, 26; P. 75, Nos. 1, 4, 10; P. 139, Nos. 12,
14.

DIVISION.

1. Give meaning to dividend, divisor, quotient, numerator,
denominator, factor.

2. Principles:—What is the effect on the quotient or the
fraction, (1) of multiplying or dividing the dividend or the
numerator, (2) of multiplying or dividing the divisor or the
denominator, (3) of multiplying or dividing both?

3. Bring practical examples to illustrate these problems:—
(1) dividend and divisor given, to find the quotient; (2) divi-
dendend and quotient given, to find the divisor; (3) quotient
and divisor given, to find the dividend.

.4 Explain these exercises:—(1) 867÷24; (2)847÷27
(3) 9678÷472; (4) 500÷005; (5) 67÷3-7; (6) 25-28÷
3-4 (7) Divide 2 gal. 2 qt. 1 pt. by 15; (8) 85 rods is what
decimal of a mile?

5. Explain the process of cancellation. Upon what principle
does it depend?

6. Solve the following practice exercises:—P. 78, Nos. 21,
22, 27. Page 13, Nos. 3, 6, 8, 10.

7. By selling a farm of 275 acres for $1360, I gained $900.
How much did I pay for the farm?

8. The bottom of a cistern measures 8 ft. 6 in. by 2 ft. 4
in. How deep must it be to contain 80 cubic feet?

9. Bring in the written solution to the following:—P. 114,
Nos. 41, 45; P. 165, Nos. 1, 3, 6, 10, 11.

DIVISORS AND MULTIPLIES

1. Give the meaning to prime factor, composite factor, L. C. M., G. C. D.

2. How can you tell when numbers are disible by 2, 3, 4, 5, 8?

3. Resolve into prime factors 96, 684, 4305, 1331, 68364.

4. Through your knowledge of the multiplication table, factor all the numbers to 100 by inspection.

5. By factoring, find the L. C. M. and G. C. D. of the following:—(1) 144, 264, 540; (2) 240, 336, 480; (3) 81, 117, 126, 135.

6. Solve the following exercises of the text:—Ex. 115, 1 to 10,; P. 65, 3 to 10.

FRACTIONAL REDUCTIONS.

1. Give meaning of mixed number, proper fraction, improper fractions, compound fraction, complex fraction.

2. State the principle of all reduction of numbers. What is its object? When is an expression in its simplest form?

3. Changed to whole or mixed numbers:—9-2, 45-12, 3137-45, 12412-151.

4. Change 13 to 6ths, 31 to 24ths.

5. Change to improper fractions:—10 7-8, 40 7-15, 127 2-35.

6. Change to the lowest terms:—9-135, 308-176, 66-1046.

7. Change to least common denominator:—4-5, 2-9, and 14-15; 7-12, 9-20, and 19-30.

8. Arrange 7-10, 3-5 and 2-3 in the order of their magnitude. Which is the greater $7-8 or $8-9?

9. Reduce to the simplest forms:—10-21x1-8x2 1-7; 1 3-4 divided by 17 1-4.

10. Change to common fractions:—.25, .425, .05, .78, .54.

11. Change to decimal fractions:—7-8, 9-10, 24-16, 9-25, 11-125.

12. Solve:—.2x7-9-:-1.15—3-5.

13. Bring in these exercises from the text:—P. 82, Nos. 7, 11, 13, 15: P. 63, Nos. 8, 11, 12: P. 122, Nos. 7, 12, 21: P. 123, Nos. 13, 15, 20, 21.

14. Find the fractional equivalent of 5-13 having a denominator of 39.

15. If 2 were added to a certain number, 5-8 of the sum would be 40. Find the number.

DENOMINATE REDUCTION

1. Standards of measurement:—1) Commit and recite the tables of length, area, volume, capacity, weight, time, money. (2) Give the standard units of each. (3) Give the derivative relation of each.

2. (1)—Illustrate the method of reduction descending and ascending; (2) Construct two problems for each table, illustrating the two kinds of reduction for each.

3. Solve the following exercises from the text:—Ex. 251, Nos. 5, 6, 10; Ex. 253, Nos. 5, 7; Ex. 254, Nos. 6, 10, 12, 14, 19; Ex. 256, Nos. 2, 5, 10, 15, 17.

4. Find the cost of 80 rods of wire fencing of four wires at 2 cents per yard.

5. How many pieces of paper, each 3 inches wide, and 4 inches long can be cut from a sheet 12 inches by 16 inches? Draw a diagram.

6. How many cubic inches are there in a cube whose edge is 4 feet?

7. A wagon is 11 feet long and 3 1-2 feet wide. How high must the wood be piled in it to make a load of 2 cords?

8. What is the value of a township of land at the rate of $4,000 for each quarter section? Draw a diagram.

9. How many feet of timber in 75 pieces of wainsscoting, each 10 feet long, 4 inches wide, and half an inch thick?

10. How many bricks are required for a double brick wall 75 feet long and 8 feet high?

11. How many bunches of shingles 4 1-2 inches to the weather will lay a shingle roof 40 feet by 28 feet?

12. Find the cost of plastering a ceiling 24 feet by 18 feet, at 9 cents a square yard.

13. Find the cost of carpeting a room 36 feet by 26 feet with carpet 3-4 of a yard wide, at 75 cents a yard.

14. How many 2 1-2 inch pickets placed 2 inches apart are required for a fence 4 rods long?

15. How many bushels of wheat will a bin 10 feet by 8 feet by 5 feet contain? How many gallons?

16. How much lumber in one gable of a barn 30 feet wide, if the roof be third-pitch?

17. A town block is 300 feet square. Find the cost of building a 4 foot sidewalk around it at 16 cents a square foot.

PERCENTAGE

1. Give meaning to the terms in percentage and show their relation to corresponding terms in the fundamental processes.

2. Express as hundredths and also as per cent:—(1) 1, 1-5, 2-5, 4-5, 1-3, 2-3, 1-4, 3-4, 1-2, 3-8, 5-8, 7-8, 1-6, 15-16, 17-19, 41-45; (2) Memorize the first fourteen of the foregoing fractions with their per cent. equivalents.

3. What fractions in their lowest terms are equivalent to the following:—4 per cent., 20 per cent., 25 per cent., 80 per cent., 75 per cent., 100 per cent., 12 1-2 per cent., 16 2-3 per cent., 120 per cent., 250 per cent., 325 per cent.?

4. Read the following decimals as per cents.: .25, .16 2-3, .75, 1.20, .37 1-2, 2.40, .001-3.

5. Solve the following problems from the text by the fractional method:—(Convert the rate into a fraction and then give the fractional analysis) : Ex. 306, Nos. 15, 22; Ex. 307, Nos. 7, 11, 17, 22, 26; Ex. 308, Nos. 5, 7; Ex. 309, Nos. 4, 5, 8; Ex. 312, Nos. 1 to 25.

COMMERCIAL TRANSACTIONS

1. Upon what is the rate of profit and loss always reckoned? Illustrate.

2. Define commission, commission merchant, broker.

3. Upon what is the commission always reckoned? Illustrate. Show the relation of the terms in commission to those of general percentage.

4. Find the amount of an agent's sales, when his commission at 5 per cent. amounts to $3765. Make other problems similiar to this one.

5. What is meant by commercial or catalogue discount? When two discounts are allowed, show the order in which they are deducted. Make problems and bring them to the class solved.

6. A commission merchant sold 200 bbl. of flour at $6 a bl. and received 4 per cent. commission. What was his commission? What did he remit to his employer? From the data

given in this problem, construct others requiring respectively the rate of commission, selling price, the remittance.

7. Bring in the solution of the following problems from the text:—P. 241, Ex. 318, Nos. 7, 9, 15, 23; P. 245, Ex. 320, Nos. 24, 27, 30, 32; P. 246, Ex. 321, Nos. 5, 7, 13, 18, 20, 22.

TAXES.

1. Explain (1) state and local taxation: (2) national taxes; (3) assessment, specific duty, ad valorem duty.

2. What is the rate of taxation in the town where the institute is held? Enumerate the various sources which make up this rate. A's house is valued at $1,600. How much does he pay to the territory? To the county? For school purposes?

3. I build a house for $1,500; the tax is 5 mills on the dollar, the property being valued at 2-3 its value or cost. Leaving out repairs and insurance, at how much must I rent the house to realize 10 per cent. a year on my money? .

4. Silver City wishes to build a school house costing $30,000. The property of the town is valued at $500,000. If the bonds run for 30 years, what should be the annual levy to create a sinking fund for the redemption at the end of the period?

5. Bring in the solution to the following problems:—P. 276, Ex. 356, Nos. 1, 2, 3, 4, 5, 9, 11, 12.

INTEREST

1. Through a solution of a problem develop interest, principal, amount and rate of interest.

2. To find the interest of any sum at any rate for any length of time, multiply the principal by the rate and this product by the time in years and the fractional part of a year. The fractional part of a year will be as many 360ths as the number of months reduced to days plus the days. By this rule, solve the following problems from the text:—P. 251, Ex. 324, Nos. 5, 8, 9; Ex. 325, Nos. 4, 6, 10.

3. Find the amount of $385 from June 7, 1907, to October 13, 1909, at 6 1-2 per cent.

RATIO AND PROPORTION

1. Give meaning to the terms ratio, proportion, antecedent, consequent, means, extremes. .

2.   What are the tests for a true ratio? For a true proportion?

3.   Solve and explain both by proportion and analysis the
following problems:—P. 317, Ex. 401, Nos. 3, 7, 8, 10, 14,
16.

5.   Explain the nature of stocks. Bring solutions to these
problems:—P. 369, Ex. 471, Nos. 4, 7, 8, 11, 13.

REVIEW PROBLEMS

1.   Solve the review problems from P. 292 to P. 310 and
from P. 325 to P. 328. Use both oral and written explanations
of those in articles 389 and 390. See that the language is gram-
matical and agrees with that of the problem. A variety of forms
is allowable, but be sure to guide in the direction of the best.
In dealing with the written problems, teach the best forms of
solution.

ELEMENTARY ENGLISH LANGUAGE AND GRAMMAR

In the following outlines, Reed and Kellogg's Graded Lessons in English is the text used as a basis. The figures in
parentheses refer to lessons in that book. For exercises, the
instructor should select only the simplest necessary to illustrate
the points under consideration.

LESSON I.

A brief discussion of thought and its expression by words,
(1, 2, 3). The simple statement of a complete thought, *Boys
run.* The sentence (4). Subject and predicate (6, 7, 11).
Nouns (14). Pronouns (19). Verbs (16). Ten sentences to
be analyzed and words parsed. (Show that diagrams are a
means and not an end, and should be used only to illustrate
analysis.)
Composition: (8, 9).
Proper use of *is* and *are, was* and *were.*

LESSON II.

The large boys run swiftly. The modified subject (20). The
modified predicate (24). Adjectives (22). Adverbs (27). Ten
sentences to be analyzed, and words parsed.
Composition: (29, 30).
Proper use of *has* and *have, did* and *done.*

LESSON III.

The large boys in the yard run swiftly to the well. Phrase
(31). Prepositions and prepositional phrases (31, 34). Illustrate the use of conjunctions and interjections (36). Ten sentences to be analyzed and words parsed.

Composition: (4).

Proper use of *saw* and *seen, wrote* and *written.*

LESSON IV. .

Any language, Latin, German, Spanish, or English, uses
eight groups or classes of words called Parts of Speech—
nouns, pronouns, verbs, adjectives, adverbs, prepositions, conjunctions and interjections and classifying the words in many
sentences (1-40).

Composition: (37, 40).

Proper use of *spoke* and *spoken, came* and *come, went* and
gone.

LESSON V. .

Classify sentences according to meaning—declarative, interrogative, imperative (63). Show how each of these may become and exclamatory sentence. Analyze and parse sentences
in (64). Diagram four.

Composition: (63).

Proper use of *set* and *sit, lay* and *lie, raise* and *rise.*

LESSON VI.

Review the simple sentence. subject and predicate. Teach
compound subject and compound predicate (35). Classify sentences according to form—simple, complex (57). and compound (62). Analyze and parse sentences in (65). Diagram
four. Classify first as to form and then as to meaning.

Composition: (67, 68).

LESSON VII.

Complements—attribute, objective and object (39, 82). Compound complements. Select five sentences each from the text,
illustrating attribute, objective, and object complements. Better still, make original sentences. Analyze and diagram sentences. Parse words used in the sentences.

Composition: Write a short story, taking some incident from
personal experience as the subject.

Lesson VIII.

Review classification of sentences as to form,—studying complex sentences carefully (57). Adjective clause (58). Adverb clause (59). Noun clause (61). Analyze and diagram sentences in (57, 59, 61).

Lesson IX.

Nouns: Common and proper (71). Five uses in sentences (6, 34, 39, 82). Number (78, 79). Gender (80). Case (81, 83). Abundant material for parsing will be found in lessons indicated. See model in (86).

Lesson X.

Pronouns: Uses in the sentences. Classify as personal, relative, interrogative, adjective (71, 72). For modifications of pronouns see (78, 79, 80, 81. 82, 83). Abundant material for parsing will be found in these lessons. See model in (86).

Proper use of *I, he, she, they, who, me, him, her, them, whom,* (85). See model in (86).

Lesson XI.

Adjectives: Descriptive and definitive (73). Comparison (81, 88). Abundant material for parsing will be found in lessons indicated.

Lesson XII.

Adverbs: Classified acording as they express time. manner, place, degree (75). Comparison (87, 88). Find material for practice in (87, 88).

Proper use of *good* and *well* and of the double negative.

Lesson XIII.

Conjunctions (35, 36): Co-ordinate, subordinate (76). List of connectives. Relative pronouns and conjunctive adverbs used as connectives. Make original complex and compound sentences and sentences containing compound elements to illustrate the use of connectives.

Proper use of *as* and *as if* instead of *like.*

LESSON XIV.

Prepositions and interjections (34, 36, 41) : Find model for written parsing adapted to all parts of speech on P. 271, and use daily in this and the remaining lessons. Analyze and diagram eight sentences in (100) and parse words.

LESSON XV.

Verbs: Uses; predicate (6, 16), participles and infinitives (48, 49). Classes: form (74, 91) ; meaning (74).

Define conjugation, synopsis, principal parts; and learn principal parts of verbs in (91).

Analyze and diagram four sentences in (100) and parse words.

LESSON XVI.

Verbs: Modifications; voice (89), mode (90, 94), tense (90, 94), number (90, 92-95)(person (90, 92-95). If the instructor thinks best, consideration of the subjunctive and potential modes may be omitted.

Learn the conjugation of the verbs *see, be, walk, write.*

Agreement of the verb (95). Errors in the form of the verb (96).

Analyze and diagram four sentences in (100) and parse words. For a model for written parsing of verbs, see (97).

LESSON XVII.

Verbs: Review (6, 16, 48, 49, 74, 89, 90, 91, 92, 93, 94, 95, 96, 98).

Make a special study of infinitives and participles as verbal noun and adjectives, (48, 49, 50) ; also study them as belonging to the verb (90-94, 96, 98). Find material for analyzing in (48, 49).

Analyze and diagram four sentences in (100), and parse all words.

LESSON XVIII.

Letter writing (229-243). Why does letter writing serve as a good composition exercise?

Let each member of the institute hand in a letter, asking for a position.

For rules of punctuation in composition work, refer to pp. 224-229.

Lesson XIX.

Review : pp. 247-266.

Write an essay of two hundred words on "The School House and Its Surroundings", being careful as to punctuation and capitalization (100).

Analyze each sentence and parse two words of each Part of Speech found in the essay.

Lesson XX.

Let the instructor take up the period reading letters and compositions of the two preceding days, indicating errors and good points. Impress the fact that the study of grammar should lead to ability in correct expression of ideas.

Geography

The figures in parentheses refer to pages of the adopted text Natural Introductory Geography, a copy of which should be in the hands of each member of the institute.

LESSON I.

Have the members of the institute make a plan of the school room on a definite scale, locating certain specified objects in the room. In like manner have a plan made of the school yard or other outside enclosure. Secure a map of the county and locate cities, towns, villages, and rural schools. Enter also mountains, streams, railroads, and main wagon roads. Make note of elevations, lowlands, climate, animal and plant life, occupation of the people, products and commerce of the county. Think of the county as a part of New Mexico; New Mexico as a part of the United States; the United States as a part of North America; North America as one of the land divisions of the earth. At this point introduce a globe, if one can be secured. Locate on it North America, the United States, New Mexico, the county where the institute is being held. By the use of the globe illustrate the movements of the earth and their results. Explain: axis, poles, equator, zones. Compare the appearance of North America on the globe with its appearance on the map in the text. (1-20).

LESSON II.

Review Lesson I.

"Geography teaches about the world in which we live; what places and things there are in it, where they are and how they are useful to man."

"Geography is the study of the earth as the home of man."

Discuss these statements.

Name the races of mankind and the homes of each.

Give the general characteristics of each race and discuss their respective stages of civilization. Study especially the races on the continent of America. (1-20).

Have prepared a list of supplementary books for use in teaching geography. Let teachers submit lists and suggest others.

LESSON III.

North America—Study acording to the following topical outline (Illinois Course of Study).

1. Location, size, and outline.
   Coast features, large islands.
2. Surface.
   Highlands, mountains; lowlands, rivers.
3. Climate.
   Hot belts, temperate belts, cold belts.
   Prevailing winds, rainfall.
4. Life.
   Forests, grassy plains, deserts.
   Animals, wild and domestic.
   People, noting progress in education especiallv.
5. Industry and Commerce.
   Chief productions.
   Routes of commerce.
   Great cities (including capitals).

Let each member of the institute make a rough outline map of North America and learn and enter fifty place names, including the largest gulfs and bays, peninsulas, capes, islands, mountains, lakes, rivers, cities, railroads. Mark the main political divisions. Indicate in a general way, where each of the chief products is found and where population is dense. Regions of rainfall should be noted as well as the elevation of different sections. (21-29).

LESSON IV.

South America.—Follow outlines and suggestions given in Lesson III for North America. (74-85).

LESSON V.

South America.—Lesson IV, continued (74-85).

LESSON VI.

Eurasia.—Follow outlines and suggestions given in Lesson III, for North America. (86-125).

LESSON VII.

Europe.—Follow outlines and suggestions given in Lesson III, for North America. (89-111).

LESSON VIII.

Europe—Lesson VI. continued. (89-111).

LESSON IX.

Europe.—Lessons VI. and VII., continued. (89-111).

LESSON X.

Asia.—Follow outlines and suggestions given in Lesson III, for North America. (112-125).

LESSON XI.

Asia.—Lesson IX, continued. (112-125).

LESSON XII.

Africa.—Follow outlines and suggestions given in Lesson III, for North America. (126-136).

LESSON XIII.

Africa.—Lesson XI continued. (126-136).

LESSON XIV.

Australia and the Pacific Islands.—Follow outlines and suggestions given in Lesson III, for North America. (137-142).

LESSON XV.

Review Lesson III.

Compare North America with other grand divisions as to area, form, etc. Study it more closely, noting its main political divisions, Canada, United States, Mexico, Central America (especially Panama-isthmus and canal). Study each division as to location, size, outline, surface, climate, plant and animal

life, history, government, occupations and commerce of the
people. Note especially: chief productions, large mountains and
rivers, and chief cities, with connecting routes. Show the relation of the United States to each of the other countries·of North
America. (20-29).

Lesson XVI.

The United States—Northeastern section. (30-41 and 42-
45).
Draw a careful outline map of the United States and indicate highlands and lowlands, rainfall, cotton region, wheat
region, potato region, forest region, coal fields, large rivers,
chief cities (15) and main railroads.
Let the instructor form an outline for the study of the northeastern section and for each section in the lessons following.
Make an outline which will serve for all sections. Indicate
characteristics peculiar to each section.

Lesson XVII.

The United States.—Northern Section. (30-41 and 46-55).

Lesson XVIII.

The United States.—Southern Section. (30-41 and 56-61).

Lesson XIX.

The United States.—Plateau and Pacific Sections. (30-41
and 61-67).
  Insular possessions.

Lesson XX.

New Mexico.—For a more complete outline of New Mexico,
see Geography, Part I. Exploration and occupation by the
Spaniards. Spanish names. Early and later Indian inhabitants.
Indian names. Difficulties in the path of early settlers. The
Santa Fe Trail. The coming of the railway. Find a few facts
concerning the geological history of the Southwest to explain
its surface, soil, climate, lack of vegetation. Compare elevation, rainfall, forests, population, occupations and products of
the different sections of the territory. Locate agricultural, mining, lumbering, grazing sections and account for each. Locate

the Forest Reserves. Name places of great historic or romantic interest.

Draw outline map of New Mexico and name contiguous states. Enter county seats and other principal cities, mountain ranges, rivers, lines of railroad. Indicate the location of the University of New Mexico, College of Agriculture and Mechanic Arts, Normal University, Normal School, Spanish Normal, Military Institute, School of Mines, School for Deaf and Dumb, and the School for the Blind. Write in the names of counties so as to indicate their relative positions.

Compare New Mexico with other states and territories as to area, population, products, miles of railway. Make a special study of its stage in the development of education as compared with those of other states.

Home county (in which the institute is being held) ; Make a study of the map used in Lesson I. Note the county's area, surface, outline, contiguous counties, county seat and other cities and towns, railroads, streams, roads, mountains, population, occupations, products. Make a special study of its educational facilities and its educational progress as compared with that of other counties (see Bienniel Report for 1907-1908 by the Territorial Superintendent of Public Instruction)

Orthography

In the following outlines sufficient material is given for use in the four weeks' institute. Each member of the institute should have the adopted text, Reed's Word Lessons, and Webster's Common School Dictionary. The figures in parentheses refer to the lessons in the adopted text. It is suggested that pages 3 to 6 inclusive be read and discussed from time to time. Seriously consider the question, "How may spelling be taught in the school so as to secure the best results"?

In written lessons, the instructor should pronounce each word distinctly. Pronounce no word more than twice.

Study also Hodgin's "Study of Spoken Language."

(In Examination Words For Spelling Will be Selected From Lessons 1-90.)

Lesson I.

Elementary sounds; letters of the alphabet; vowels, consonants. Define each.

Diacritical markings: need of; illustrate, macron, breve, dieresis or dots above or below, semi-dieresis or dot above or below, cedilla, caret or circumflex, tilde, suspended bar, transverse bar, modified macron. Make a table of all diacritical markings for a , e, i, o, u, y, c, n, s, x, ch and th; for example a with a macron as in *ate,* g with a dot above as in *gem..* Be sure that the sound represented is made clear.

Study carefully (30, 82, 83, 84).

Lesson II.

Lesson 1. Reviewed.

Lesson III.

Drill on table of diacritical markings.

Mark, pronounce, spell, and define: trace, case, praise, stray, badge, spasm, catch, eye, black, near, queer, debt, death, blithe, scythe, bridge, yolk, hoarse, mourn, owe, knob, knock, use, cube, news, buzz, dumb. (1-7).

Illustrate from the foregoing: vowel, consonant, syllable, monosyllable, primitive word.

Lesson IV.

Homonyms (in this and following lessons on homonyms, the instructor should dictate exercises from text requiring members of the institute to use the right word); pain, pane; be, bee; blew, blue; him, hymn; knot, not; maid, made; knew, new; cent, scent, sent. (9-19).

Synonyms (in this and following lessons on synonyms, the members of the institute should be required to write original sentences as an exercise in the right use of synonyms): bring, fetch; haste, hurry; idle, indolent, lazy; content, satisfied. (Part IV).

Define: root, primitive word, derivative words, compound words; affix, prefix, suffix.

Rule I.—Final e is dropped before a vowel (107). Note some exceptions in (120).

Lesson V.

Drill on table of diacritical markings.

Mark, pronounce, spell, and define: half, jar, gape, haunt, talk, false, faults, gnaw, last, dance, task, scare, chair, swear tomb, smooth, spruce, group, wound, full, soot, push, purr, word, err, stern, stir, thirst, voice, clay, cloud crowd. (11-17).

Lesson VI.

Homonyms: ate, eight; hart, heart; all, awl; stare, stair; read, reed; read, red; die, dye; fore, four; forth, fourth; to, too, two; threw, through; sun, son; wood, would; earn, urn. (18-19).

Synonyms: clumsy, awkward; error; mistake, blunder; discover, invent; genius, talent; courage, bravery, fortitude, heroism. Part IV.

Word building: Form words with prefixes un-, dis-, mis-, and note the force of the prefix as affecting the word to which it is joined. (95).

Rule II.—In monosyllables and words accented on the last syllable, a final consonant after a single vowel doubles before a suffix beginning with a vowl (*x, k* and *v* are never doubled). (109). Note exceptions in (122).

LESSON VII.

Review table of diacritical markings.

Mark, pronounce, spell, and define: leaf, fierce, again, many, flight, eye, aisle, prince, busy, been, women, bowl, gourd, sew, beau, prompt, watch, scrap, bruise, chew, beauty, front, touch, wool, bosom, could, verge, world, heard, myrtle. (20-25).

Define and illustrate from the foregoing: vocal equivalents, syllable, monosyllable, dissyllable, syllabicate or syllabify, accent.

LESSON VIII.

Homonyms: gate, gait; grate, great; hail, hale; bare, bear; pare, pear, pear; ale, ail; mane, main; pause, paws. (27-29).

Review the ground covered during the previous days.

Rule III.—*y* after a consonant becomes *i* before a suffix not beginning with *i*. (III). Note exceptions in (123).

LESSON IX.

Synonyms: cheerfulness, gayety, mirth; comfort, consolation, solace; silent, taciturn; cloister, monastery, nunnery, priory or abbey. (Part IV).

Word building: Form words with suffixes -ed, -er, -est, -ing, -ish, -able and -ible, -full, and note the force of the suffix as affecting the word to which it is joined. (97).

Abbreviations: states, months, days, names and titles, business terms. (72-76).

Study rules for forming plurals of nouns. (124-126).

LESSON X.

Review table of diacritical markings.

Mark, syllabicate, accent, pronounce, spell, and define: blaze, trait, lapse, charge, bold, blanch, spare, nymph, bronze, soup, choose, nudge, urge, squad, their, prayer, obey, jerk, germ, police, dirt, tongue, cork, wolf, worse, worth, brook, rude, fruit, rythm. (32-33).

Pronunciation: aunt, ant, psalm, almond, pastor, off, dog,

cloth, gone, duke, mule, Tuesday, sure. (31-34).

Synonyms: abstinence, temperance; famous, illustrious; noted, notorious; poverty, indigence; murder, assassinate. (Part IV).

LESSON XI.

Dictation: Let the instructor dictate some well known poem and require correct spelling and pronunciation. Write it correctly on the blackboard and require members of the institute to make correction in their respective exercises.

Review rules and definitions used in previous·lessons.

Pronounce: America, sofa, draw, idea, cow, widow, talking, evening, government, ignorance, often, golden, shovel, hyphen, quarrel, shrub, bands, builds, facts, beasts, ever, library. (104 135).

LESSON XII.

Hyomonyms: stake, steak; wait, weight; waste, waist; reign, rein, rain; tacks, tax; beat, beet; beer, bier; dear, deer; feat, feet; key, quay; knead, need. (35, 36).

Synonyms: narrative, description; defended, protected; recovery, restoration; difference, distinction; definition, explanation; sure, certain. (Part IV).

Word building: Form words with suffixes -ly, -ness, -less, -en, -ous, -s or -es, and 's, and note the force of the suffix as affecting the word to which it is joined. (99).

Learn rules for making the possessive forms of nouns. (124-127).

LESSON XIII.

Mark, syllabicate, accent, pronounce, spell, and define: owl, wren, quail, pigeon, parrot, swallow, oriole, nightingale, warble, whistle, migrate, plumage, feathers. (44-45).

Homonyms: meat, meet, mete; peace, piece; peal, peel; bread, bred; cell, sell; lead, led; berry, bury; one, won; beau, bow; been, bin; choose, chews; berth, birth; bough, bow; coarse, course. (37-39).

LESSON XIV.

Synonyms: durable, lasting, permanent; obstruction, obstacle; elegance, grace; scrupulous, conscientious.

Word building: Join affixes to the following and note the effect, love, man. Make words by adding suffixes to the root *duc*. Give ten compound words.

Misused words (illustrate correct use): love, like; awfully, very; learn, teach; elegant, delightful; lovely, pretty, pleasant; funny, strange; stay, stop; splendid, excellent; can, may.

Rule for spelling.—

> *i* before *e*
> Except after *c*
> Or when sounded as *a*
> As in neighbor or weigh.

LESSON XV.

Mark, syllabicate, accent, pronounce, spell, and define: larynx, knuckle, forehead, mustache, ribbon, handkerchief, mutton, venison, sardine, cucumber, celery, asparagus, banana, chestnut, nectarine, almond, toast, salad, omelet, succotash; doughnut, ginger, sugar, yeast, hominy, molasses, victual. (46-53).

Homonyms: dew, due; doe, dough; flew, flue; flour, flower; fowl, foul: gilt, guilt; groan, grown; heard, herd; holy, wholly; kill, kiln; knight, night; know, no; lie, lye; sea, see; son, sun; weak, week. (40-41).

Punctuation, capitalization, and other ordinary rules (see Reed and Kellogg's Graded Lessons in English, pp. 224-229).

LESSON XVI.

Misused words: expect, suppose; reckon, believe; ladies, women; gentlemen, men; locate, settle; calculate, believe; likely, intend; perpetually, continually; anticipate, expect; guess, think; balance, remainder. (168).

Abbreviations: study 170, 171, 172.

Mark, syllabicate, accent, pronounce, spell, and define: balk, neigh, whinney, gallop, girth, carriage, surcingle, pommel, mamma, papa, aunt, daughter, nephew, breeze, tempest, hurricane, cyclone, tornado, curb, area, mayor, avenue, precinct, tenement, museum, cathedral, metropolis, restaurant, aqueduct, reservoir. (54-56).

Lesson XVII.

Misused words: residence, house; reside, live; section, neighborhood; propose, purpose; recommend, advise; contemptible, contemptuous; dangerous, in danger; universal, general; posted, informed; most, almost. (169).

Synonyms: beautiful, handsome, pretty; harmony, melody; character, reputation; plurality, majority; rebellion, revolt; assent, consent; should, ought. (Part IV).

Mark, syllabicate, accent, pronounce, spell and define: laths, iron, cement, plane, trowel, hatchet, compass, giraffe, antelope, elephant, rhinoceros, popular, catalpa, mahogany, sycamore, fountain, cascade, purl foam, seethe, turbid, transparent, field, briers, meadow, precipice, cottage, orchard, hoe, plough, trough granary, arable, tillable, gypsum, phosphate, swath. (57-68).

Lesson XVIII.

Honmonyms: load, lode; right, rite, wright, write; seam, seem; rowed, rode, road; soar, sore; strait, straight; moan, mown; none, nun; ode, owed; plane, plain; pore, pour; rays, raise. (138).

Review Lessons I-IX.

Synonyms: habit, custom; memory, recollection, remembrance; understand, comprehend; education, instruction; avenge, revenge. (Part IV).

Lesson XIX.

Word building: Illustrate from these outlines; root, derivative word, compound word. Select ten derivative words and show how each is made up.

Review Lessons IX-XVIII.

Mark, syllabicate, accent, pronounce, spell, and define: cylinder, coral, chorus, charity, machine, caution, especial, mission, sugar, gossip, engine, grudge, noisy, hunger, examine, expel, pleasure, whittle, quote, cipher, laughter. (85-90).

Lesson XX.

Review definitions.
Review table of diacritical markings.
Review homonyms.
Review synonyms.

Review rules of pronunciation.

Review exercises in word building.

Review rules for spelling.

Let the instructor give out a list of 25 common words, pronouncing each word distinctly. Pronounce no word more than twice.

Physiology

(This course of lessons is based on Conn's Introductory Physiology and Hygiene .References are made to chapters. Every member of the institute should have a copy of the text.

The instructor may give supplementary material from Conn's Elementary Physiology and Hygiene. Attention is called to Outlines on Advanced Physiology and Physical Training, also this Manual).

Lesson I.

1. Show the similarity between a steam engine and the human body as to fuel, food, care.

2. What must a person know before he can be trusted to run a steam engine?

3. Is it as important that a person should early learn to properly care for and to manage his own body? Give three reasons for your answer.

4. Give three uses of food.

5. Name the best foods for children, for middle age and old age.

6. Make out a good bill of fare for breakfast, for dinner, for supper, or evening dinner.

7. Name some good animal foods, mineral foods, vegetable foods. (1-4).

Lesson II.

1. Give three reasons why people need to drink.

2. How much should a grown person drink each day?

3. Where can the best drinking water be obtained?

4. Why is some water no good for drinking purposes?

5. Are there any objections to children's drinking tea or coffee? Give reasons.

6. Name the good and bad effects of alcoholic drinks.

7. According to government statistics, alcoholic drinks cost the people of the United States more than all the flour, meat, sugar, coffee, tea, shoes, cotton, silk and woolen goods, all put together. In return for this enormous outlay, what do the people get?

8. Find out from your judges what per cent of the criminals of New Mexico were made so by alcoholic drinks.

9. Also find out from them how many thousand dollars are spent each year in trying criminal cases, and compare it with the amount spent in New Mexico for paying the teachers of the public schools. (5, 6).

Lesson III.

1. Give uses of cooking, ways of cooking, and importance of good cooking in contrast with poor cooking.

2. Write a list of meats that are improved by cooking.

3. Write a list of grains that are improved by cooking.

4. Write a list of fruits that are improved by cooking.

5. Write a list of fruits that are not improved by cooking.

6. Give four good rules about eating.

7. Should people have the same kinds of food in summer as they have in winter? Give reasons for your answer.

8. Should out-door laboring men eat any different foods in quantity or kind than do in-door clerks and professional men? Give reasons for your answer. (7-8).

Lesson IV.

1. Define digestion and name the organs of digestion in order.

2. Make a drawing of the digestive organs from the illustration on page 46.

3. Be prepared to make the drawing from memory in class and indicate the name of each organ.

4. Give the name of the digestive fluids.

5. Note carefully the villi and their work.

6. Describe the process of digestion clearly. (9).

Lesson V.

1. Name six foods very easy of digestion.

2. Name six foods that are less easy of digestion.

3. Name six that are hard to digest.

4. Write a list of what would be a good dinner for a boy or girl.

5. What is dyspepsia? By what is it often caused?

6. Describe the formation of a tooth.

7. Name the different kinds of teeth.

8. Tell how to properly care for the teeth. (10, 11).

Lesson VI.

1. Locate the heart. Give its size, shape and uses.

2. What is a "Tobacco Heart?" Tell what causes it.

3. What is "The Pulse?" What use do physicians make of the pulse?

4. Should every person learn to count his own pulse? Why?

5. Have each member tell how many times his or her pulse beats per minute.

6. Give the distinction between arteries and veins. In which is the pulse found?

7. What are the capillaries?

8. How does the blood circulate?

9. Give uses of red and white corpuscles.

10. What effect has alcohol on the blood vessels? (12).

Lesson VII.

1. Make a diagram illustrating the circulation of the blood.

2. Give uses of the circulation of the blood.

3. The temperature of a human body.

4. Where does the blood get the air to carry to various parts of the body?

5. Effect of exercise on the circulation.

6. Cuts and wounds and how to treat them.

7. How can you tell whether an artery or a vein is cut?

8. How can bleeding be stopped?

9. What is meant by the blood clot? (13, 14).

Lesson VIII.

1. Explain *why* and *how* you breathe.

2. Which is better, to breathe through the nose or the mouth? Give reasons for your answer.

3. Make a drawing of the "Breathing Tree," and explain it.

4. Why does the blood go to the lungs? What change takes place there? (15, 16).

LESSON IX.

1. Discuss the need of outdoor exercise.
2. Games, best suited for physical training.
3. Discuss the need of ventilation.
4. How may your school room be ventilated? Discuss at length.
5. How many cubic feet of air should a person have every minute? (17).

LESSON X.

1. What is the skeleton? Give three uses.
2. Describe the formation of a bone. Approximate number of bones.
3. What is the backbone, the spinal cord, the skull, the ribs, the ligaments?
4. Describe the different kinds of joints.
5. Speak about the growth of the bones.
6. Tell how the body may be made and kept graceful.
7. Describe and give the remedy for a dislocation, a sprain, a fracture. (18, 19).

LESSON XI.

1. What are the muscles?
2. Describe their formation.
3. Voluntary and Involuntary muscles.
4. Tendons.
5. How may the muscles be strengthened?
6. What effect has alcohol on the muscles?
7. Using the muscles. The effect of exercise. (20, 21).

LESSON XII.

1. Describe the skin and give the three uses of the skin.
2. What are pores, sweat glands? Give their uses.
3. Give different ways of caring for the skin and finger nails.

4.   Give ways in which the skin may be injured.

5.   How should corns and warts be treated? (22, 24).

LESSON XIII.

1.   Describe the brain as to size and location.

2.   What are convolutions?

3.   Make a drawing of the brain to show its shape and parts.

4.   Name and discuss three duties of the brain.

5.   Discuss the activity of the brain.

6.   What effect has alcohol on the brain?

7.   What effect does the use of beer have on children?

8.   What effect does the use of cigarettes and tobacco have on boys?

9.   What effect does work have on the brain?

10.   Speak of the need of rest for the brain. (25, 26).

LESSON XIV.

1.   What are the brain messengers? What do those messengers tell us?

2.   Name and give the function of two general kinds of nerves.

3.   Name the five senses and give the organ of each.

4.   Speak about the senses of touch, hearing, taste, smell, and a nerve for each. Show how we feel, hear, taste, smell.

5.   Make a diagram of the hearing apparatus so as to be able to reproduce it from memory. (27).

LESSON XV.

1.   Read what is said about the sense of sight in Chapter 27.

2.   Name the parts of the eye.

3. - Make a diagram of the eye and indicate the parts. Be prepared to reproduce the diagram from memory.

4.   Tell how the eyes may best be cared for. What should be avoided?

5.   Nearsightedness.

6.   Why is it necessary to cultivate the voice?

7.   How are sounds made? The vocal cords.

8.   How are words made?

9.   Tell how to care for the voice. (28, 29).

LESSON XVI.

1. How are diseases taken?
2. Describe the symptoms of measles, chicken pox, whooping cough, mumps, scarlet fever, diptheria, smallpox. Give some directions as to treatment of each .
3. Diseases carried through the air, typhoid fever, "La Grippe," consumption. Germs.
4. What is the best way to avoid catching diseases? (30).

LESSON XVII.

1. What is a citizen?
2. Why do we have laws and officers?
3. The Board of Health and its duties.
4. Importance of public cleanliness.
5. What should be done with garbage?
6. The necessity of having pure water.
7. How may diseases be kept from spreading?
8. Consumption or Tuberculosis. How may it be checked? (31).

LESSON XVIII.

1. Cleanliness in housekeeping.
2. How should rooms be furnished so as to keep out dirt and germs most easily?
3. Give some hints as to dusting, sweeping, dishwashing.
4. Danger from flies and mosquitos.
5. Odors and disinfectants. What and why used?
6. How should cellars and yards be kept clean?
7. How may home be made the happiest? (32).

LESSON XIX.

1. What should be done in the case of stings or bites from insects, from animals, from snakes?
2. What should be done if poison has been swallowed?
5. Give remedies for burns, frostbites, fainting ,nose bleed, bruises, headache, earache, colds, sore throat.
4. What should be done if something gets into the ear, nose or throat?
5. Describe a household medicine cupboard, how to make one, tell what should be put into it. (33, 34).

LESSON XX.

1. Self government means temperance in all things.
2. Early to bed.
3. Controlling the appetite.
4. Playing too long.
5. Controlling the temper.
6. Learn and memorize twelve everyday rules of health. (35, 36).

Penmanship

The following outlines contain much 'that is suggested by the 1906 course of study for Normal Institutes of Kansas and the 1906-07 Manual and Course of Study of the Albuquerque City Schools. The course is intended to cover the entire subject of penmanship concisely, to illustrate the proper method of conducting the writing exercises of the school and also to afford those who need it some opportunity for improving their writing. Let the instructor devote ten minutes of each day to the discussion of questions relating to the teaching of penmanship ten minutes to teaching lessons and drilling class in unison on movement exercises and on letters and words, and ten minutes for individual practice and advancement in the regular course. In the individual practice each one writes each exercise until his work is approved by the instructor. Pages of words should be kept by the members of the institute as specimens and to mark the advancement in the course. These pages should have the writer's name and the instructor's mark of approval on them. Each member of the institute should be provided with pen and ink and good paper; also with the series of Ginn and Co's Medial Writing Books. The instructor should secure the Manual which accompanies the series. Note also Lessons XIV and XV following.

LESSON I.

What need is there of careful attention to penmanship in the schools? A definite system of letter forms has been adopted for the schools of New Mexico and all teachers must teach by this system. Why? Discuss the Medial Writing Books series adopted.

Have each member of the institute hand in an exercise dictated by the instructor to show his best handwriting.

Lesson II.

Position of the body. Position of the book. Position of the hand and pen. Follow directions given inside the first cover of the Medial Writing Books. Teach these positions to the institute by considerable drill each day. Let the instructor read what is said to the teachers on the inside of the first cover.

Writing lesson: Have handed in the following exercise:
1. Place and date.
2. "This is a specimen of my best penmanship at this time."
3. The small letters.
4. The Arabic numerals.
5. The capital letters.

The instructor should criticise this exercise by commenting upon it to each individual.

Lesson III.

Movement: Discuss finger, whole arm, and forearm or muscular movement. Of what age and grade of pupils would you require each? The members of the institute should of course use the muscular movement and practice daily in and out of class on the "Movement Exercises" found on the outside of the back cover of the Mdial Writing Bks.

Writing Lesson: Practice on i, n, e, u, m, a, and write a page of words containing these letters only—for example, name, mine, immune.

Lesson IV.

Materials: Paper, pencil, pens, penholder, ink, penwiper, blotter. Discuss use and care of each.

Writing Lesson: Movement exercises (on outside of back cover of Medial Writing Books) Nos. 1, 2, 3, 4, 5; practice again on letters given in Lesson III and write page of words containing them.

Lesson V.

Discuss the desk; inclined or level, height. Review what has been learned about position of body, book, hand, and pen.

Writing Lesson: Movement exercises 1, 2, 3, 4, 5, 17, 15

and 26; practice on l, h, j, y, g, and write a page of words containing only letters that have been learned.

LESSON VI.

Form of letters: Show here that a correct mental image of the whole form is necessary. How may it be obtained?

Writing lesson: Same as in V.

Do not analyze letters. Call attention to variations from proper form.

LESSON VII.

Copy books: Let the instructor give careful suggestions as to the use of the copy book in the school room. How can one book be made to last through another term? Should one page be filled before another is begun, or are better results gained by going back for review? The copy book records only the best efforts.

LESSON VIII.

Practice books: Necessary for work preliminary to using the copy book. Exercises on practice sheet should be as neatly and carefully done as in the copy book. The pupil should record his best effort only when the copy under consideration has been written on the practice sheets to the satisfaction of the teacher.

Writing Lesson: Same as in VII.

LESSON IX.

Time: What time in the day is the best for the writing lesson? How long a period should be devoted to it?

Writing Lesson: Movement exercises Nos. 1, 2, 3, 4, 5, 6, 7, 8, 9, 10, and write a page of words containing letters used thus far.

LESSON X.

Writing for beginning pupils: Use blackboard and unruled pencil paper, and pencil. After three or four months use practice books. The child "works in a large way" at the beginning; he makes large circles, large drawings, etc., naturally. Take advantage of this by allowing him to begin at the blackboard and on unruled paper. Gradually improve the form and reduce the size of his letters. When should the child be allowed to use pen and ink?

Writing Lesson: Same as in Lesson IX.

LESSON XI.

Writing for intermediate pupils: What additional requirements should be enforced?

Writing Lesson: Movement Exercises, Nos. 1, 2, 3, 4, 17, 15, 19, 22; practice on b, k, f, z, q, and write a page of words containing letters used to date.

LESSON XII.

Writing for advanced pupils: What additional requirements should be enforced?

Writing Lesson: Same as in Lesson XI.

LESSON XIII.

Pencils, Pens, Penholders: Medium soft lead pencil (No. 2) for pupils of first, second and third grades; Esterbrook No. 761 or Eagle No. E 71 pens; holders of moderate size and rough surface. Discuss.

Writing Lesson: Movement exercise Nos. 1, 2, 27; practice on capitals N, M, , and write a page of sentences beginning with these capitals.

LESSON XIV.

Conducting the Writing Lesson:

Before presenting the lesson, make a careful study of the copy for which you are preparing. Decide upon the movement exercises best suited to the copy; the particular points to which to call attention; the special letters for comparison. With the points well in mind and the class in good position, put the movement exercise on the blackboard just as you wish it to be put on the practice sheets. Talk about the exercise with the class; point out or ask pupils to mention defects in your exercise. Be sure that the pupils have the correct mental image of what they are to reproduce. It is time then to begin the practice. It is true that we learn to do by doing, but there is such a thing as doing too much "aimless" writing and too little, well-directed "quizzing." Too many teachers hurry into the penmanship lesson. Results are not secured in this way in penmanship any more than in any other subject; in tact, the chances for sucess are much less in penmanship. Count for movement exercises and secure good military quickstep.

Writing Lesson: Same as in Lesson XIII.

LESSON XV.

Conducting Writing Lesson (Continued):

During the practice work as well as during the writing of words and sentences, the teacher should be down among the pupils giving them aid, suggestions, and copies. Different pupils need different suggestions; it is impossible to satisfactorily conduct the writing lesson from the front of the room.

If the pupil is strongly inclined to write back-hand, emphasize the slant; have him turn his paper at a greater angle with his desk. If he makes too heavy lines, look to the position of the body and the holding of the pen. If he has a stiff movement, note the arm position and see if his hand glides on the finger nails.

During the entire hour, keep everybody at work on something, the purpose of which is evident. Aimless practice brings ill results.

Writing Lesson: Practice on capitals V, U, Y, W, H, K, and write a page of sentences beginning with these.

LESSON XVI.

Care of writing materials after class exercise. Discuss.

Writing Lesson: Movement Exercises, Nos. 1, 2, 3, 7, 11, 27, and 37; practice same capitals as in XV.

LESSON XVII.

Review introductory remarks and Lessons I, II, III.

Writing Lesson. Select movement exercises and practice on C, A, G, O, D, and E, and write a page of sentences beginning with these capitals.

LESSON XVIII.

Review Lessons IV, and VIII.

Writing Lesson: Select movement exercises and practice

on I, X, Z, P, R, B, and write a page of sentences beginning with these capitals.

LESSON XIX.

Review Lessons IX-XII.

Writing Lesson: Select movement exercises and practice on I, S, L, T, F, and write a stanza or a paragraph.

LESSON XX.

Review Lessons XIII-XVI.

Writing Lesson: Same as in Lesson II.

Reading

Each member of the institute should have Brooks's Reader for the sixth year and Webster's Common School Dictionary. The outlines following intend to give actual reading lessons in which the instructor should put forth his best efforts in imparting the aim and spirit necessary in teaching this subject. Topics are suggested also for daily discussions as to methods.

(References to Sherman and Reed's Essentials of Teaching Reading are intended for the institute instructors.)

LESSON I.

What is Reading? Art of acquisition and transmission of thought—silent and oral reading. What makes it the most important branch of study? Compare it with other studies as a means of developing the mental faculties. Why is it neglected by teachers and disliked by pupils? What portion of time should be given to reading in school?

Reading Lesson: "The Good Saxon King", p. 46. Directions for preparation: Read silently. Be able to tell or write the story in your own words. What persons are named in the story? Who is the main character? Tell what each of the other persons have to do with Alfred. What places are named? Locate each with reference to the place where Alfred lived. How long ago did the events of the story take place? From what is told in the story, how did the people of that time differ from those of the present in beliefs, dress, manners, training of children? Find out some additional facts from other sources, if possible. What instances are given to show Alfred's courage, justice, industry, and resourcefulness? Define the following words, noting the meanings in connection with the sentences where the words are used: *pilgrimages,* favorite, illuminated, *diligence,* treaties, *dispersed, disguise, peasant,* cowherd, musician, minstrel, summoning, pirate, *valiantly*, foreign, *partial*, notched. Give synonymns for words in italics.

Read the story orally with correct position, breathing, and enunciation.

LESSON II.

Discuss the lesson of the previous day and let each member of the institute make an outline for study and for recitation, having in mind the two phases: (1) Word study, (2) thought study.

Reading Lesson: "The Sandpipers' Nest", pp. 71.74. Directions for preparation to be given by the instructor.

. LESSON III.

Discuss the following faults: Reading too low, reading too loud, reading too fast, reading too slowly, monotone, unnatural tones, rising inflection at close of sentence, singsong reading of poetry. Upon what is proper expression in reading based? How can the foregoing faults be corrected? See chapter XI, Sherman and Reed's Essentials of Teaching Reading.

Reading Lesson: "Black Beauty", p. 93. Directions for preparation to be given by the instructor.

LESSON IV.

Teach simple definitions and give adequate illustrations of what is meant by time, grouping, melody, force and quality in reading. (See Sherman and Reed's Essentials of Teaching Reading, Part I, pp. 3-47). As opportunity offers in the reading lessons, call attention to these properties of good reading.

Reading Lesson: "Dying in the Harness", p. 101. Directions for preparation to be given by the instructor.

LESSON V.

Primary Reading: Alphabet method; phonic method, word method, sentence method, eclectic method. Discuss each. (See Sherman and Reed's Essentials of Teaching Reading, chapter VIII, pp. 77-81).

Reading Lesson: "The Old Oaken Bucket", p. 121. Directions for preparation to be given by the instructor.

Lesson VI.

Primary Reading: Words-study lists given on pages 81-85 with accompanying discussion in Essentials of Teaching Reading.

Reading Lesson: "The Miraculous Pitcher", p. 136. Directions for preparation to be given by the instructor.

Lesson VII.

Primary Reading: Phonics (pp. 85-88, Essentials of Teaching Reading).

Reading Lesson: "The Gods of Ancient Greece", p. 167.

Lesson VIII.

Primary Reading: Study the course outlined on pp. 88, 89, of the Essentials of Teaching Reading.

Is dramatization possible in the rural schools? (pp. 89-95, Essentials of Teaching Reading).

Discuss devices to be used in teaching beginners to read.

Reading Lesson: "The Secrets of Spring", p. 181.

Lesson IX.

Division of a Reading recitation: (1) The recitation proper; (2) drilling in articulation. (3) assignment of the new lesson; (4) supplementary reading. Read chapter IX of the Essentials of Teaching Reading.

Reading Lesson: Let each member of the institute make model assignments for "Pochontas", p. 27.

Lesson X.

Conduct of class in reading:
1. Position.
    (a) Of pupils; in front of class.
    (b) Of body; erect, but easy.
    (c) Of book; why do pupils hold books improperly?
2. Concert drills.
    (a) Kinds.
    (b) Value.
    (c) Frequency.
    Discuss and illustrate all points given above.
3. Individual reading.

(a) To whom shall pupil read?

(b) Will you permit criticsm of other pupils?

(c) How will you gain correct expression from pupils?

(d) How may timidity, awkwardness and indifference be overcome?

4. Material read.

(a) Shall pupil read sentences, paragraphs, or whole selection?

(b) Shall they read words, phrases, or to punctuation marks? Why?

(c) What material is suitable for sight reading?

(d) For silent reading?

5. Teacher.

When should a teacher read a lesson to pupils?

LESSON XI.

Reading Lesson: "The Apple Blossoms", p. 194. Directions for preparations to be given by the instructor. Attention should be called to the difference between prose and poetry.

. LESSON XII.

Discuss the teaching of reading in the intermediate grades or years. What should be the teacher's aim in these years?

Reading Lesson: "The Tiger, the Brahman and the Jackal", p. 225. Directions for preparations to be given by the instructor.

LESSON XIII.

Discuss the teaching of reading in the advanced grades or years. What should be the aim here?

Reading Lesson: Let each member of the institute make an assignment of "The Tiger. the Brahman and the Jackal".

LESSON XIV.

The dictionary and how to use it. Read Chapter XIII in the Essentials of Teaching Reading.

When should the dictionary be introduced? Why should it be introduced at all? Note six principles on pp. 143, 144. Attention should be called to all parts of the dictionary, certain rules of spelling, key to pronunciation, list of abbreviations, etc. Pupils must be taught to use dictionary and the institute may well take up a period in considering how this may best be done.

LESSON XV.

Articulation: Find exercises in Chapter XVI of the Essentials of .Reading. Why do people speak distinctly? Practice and drill on consonants when weakness is shown in reading.

Reading Lesson: "The Adventures of a Shilling", p. 230. Directions for preparation to be given by the instructor.

. LESSON XVI.

Ends to be obtained in teaching of reading; how to read and what to read. What constitutes a good school text in reading? Supplementary reading—

  1.   Kinds.
  2.   Use.
  3.   Advantages.

How does the teacher create a taste for good literature? In the selection of pieces for pupils to memorize, what should be the guide for teachers?

Reading Lesson: "The Wonderful Weaver", p. 234. Directions for preparation to be given by the instructor.

LESSON XVII.

Review lesson on Primary Reading. Intermediate and Advanced Reading. Let each member of the institute group what has been learned in the form of a complete outline, and enter the same in a note book for reference in actual school work.

LESSON XVIII.

Have outlines made on: The division of the recitation, the assignment of a new lesson, plan for study, conduct of the class. All these points will have been clearly demonstrated in the institute if these lessons have been faithfully followed by the instructor and the members.

- . LESSON XIX.

Review lessons on the dictionary and articulation. Call attention to the pronouncing key and words list, and the notes, pp. 241-248.

Reading Lesson: "The Cloud", p. 239. Directions for preparation to be given by the instructor.

LESSON XX.

How does reading assist all other branches in the school room? How do all other branches serve as reading lessons? Spelling, language, and grammar, to be especially correlated with reading. Geographical and historical allusions to be fully explained in each lesson. Thus the pupil will be lead to look upon all the elements of his course as related.

· Discuss the development of a love of good literature through the teaching of reading and the effect of such a love of good literature upon the after life of the child.

Study: "The Cloud" as a piece of literature.

Part III
ADDITIONAL OUTLINES
FOR
Supplementary Work in the Institute

Suggestions on School and Class Management

By Miss Lettie Watson.

LESSON I.

PREPARATION FOR WORK

"Knowledge is Power."

Teach that only which you know. Knowledge of a subject gives a teacher confidence in herself, and gains the confidence of her pupils.

Do not rely on past preparation, but prepare today what you intend to teach tomorrow.

Be in the school room, if possible, twenty minutes before actual work with pupils begins. Have everything in order so that there will be no delays.

Open the windows and have the room at the right temperature. If maps, globes, charts, crayon, etc., are to be used, have them where it will be easy to get them. In other words "Be ready."

Remember careful and thorough preparation for the work aids wonderfully in the management of the school.

LESSON II.

"A Thing of Beauty is a Joy Forever."

How true with reference to the school grounds. If they are attractive to the child, he will always remember them with pleasure.

This might seem not to come under the teacher's line of work. To a certain extent this is true. She has no choice in choosing the location. But she can try to improve what is hers for the time being. The yard can be kept clean. Trees and shrubbery can be planted in the proper places. All this done with the help of the boys and girls. It teaches them to improve their homes and cultivates love of the beautiful.

What has this to do with the management of the school? It helps boys and girls to manage themselves. They personally will have something to do besides actual play during the hours of recreation.

. LESSON III.

(School Hygiene).

"Accuse not nature, she hath done her part; Do thou but thine."

This is one of the best aids in the management of the school. Too much stress cannot be laid upon it.

1. *Ventilation—*

Lower the windows from the top. Not enough to cause a draft on the heads of the pupils. Keep windows down all the time; the temperature being about 70 degrees. At every intermission, raise all windows.

2. *Position—*

Insist upon erect position at all times. Appeal to the pride of the pupils by telling how much better he looks when he sits straight. Have him get into the habit of sitting and standing correctly. This is not easy to accomplish. "Keep at it," is the rule that directly applies. And "Never grow weary in well doing," is the best encouragement offered.

3. *Exercise—*

Every day have a drill in physical training. It is well to have a set time for this, but that is not necessary. Have it during any period of the day if it is needed. If interest in lessons lags, or if there is a marked manifestation of restlessenss, stop mental work and give a few minutes' physical exercise.

4. *Light—*

This does not rest wholly with the teacher. She has little to do with the management of seats and placing of windows, but she can see that there is not a glare of light on the books. Also, during recitations, she can arrange the pupils so that the light will come from the right direction—i. e. over the left shoulder. Be sure to have the proper lights on the blackboards.

5. *Cleanliness*—

Last, but by no means least, under the subject of "School Hygiene" comes cleanliness. The teacher should be a living example in personal appearance. The desk, tables, and all things in the school room should be kept neat and clean. The yard should be kept free from old papers and anything that tends to make it uncleanly and disorderly.

Insist upon the personal cleanliness of the pupils. If results do not come from a talk to the school, have a few private talks. Have cleanliness of pupils if it is necessary to send them home.

LESSON IV.

(Entrance and Dismissal.)

"Order is Heaven's first law."

Have a "first bell" about four minutes before the regular time to begin work. At the beginning of this bell have pupils form lines in front of the door. The arrangements of pupils in line depends upon the entrance, the number of pupils, their size, relative number of boys and girls, etc. Then have the pupils pass in orderly and take their seats. If pupils enjoy marching, beat time for them. After they are seated and are quiet, give commands for them to hang up their wraps.

When it is time for dismissal, call for some certain position to get the attention. Then by command to turn, stand, pass, have them go out in order. It is well to have lines formed in the rooms before passing. But this depends upon the room.

This seems rather military perhaps, but the "informal way" is not successful with the majority of teachers.

Children do not know law and order. It is a teacher's duty to instill it into them.

LESSON V.

(Opening Exercises.)
"When e'er a noble deed is wrought
When e'er is spoken a noble thought,
Our hearts in glad surprise
To higher levels rise."

This is the keynote of preventing tardiness. The pupils desire to be on time.

Have the first ten minutes set apart for something entertaining. Read or tell a story. Sing bright songs. Recite appropriate memory gems. Have the little folks play a game. The older pupils will enjoy watching them have a good time.

This time must not always be spent in the same way. It will be impossible to have something different every day. But have a stock of things on hand and don't allow any of them to get dusty.

This is the period to teach the whole school history, literature, etc., by observing the special days, birthdays and anniversaries.

All these things have a tendency to make the boys and girls contented with school life. If they are happy it is easy to manage them.

LESSON VI.

(Governing Pupils.)

"Be not like a stream that brawls,
Loud with shallow waterfalls;
But in quiet self control,
Link together soul with soul."

Be impartial.   Be cheerful.
Be just.   Be kind.
Be positive.   Be firm.

The teacher is the head of the school, and the pupils must be made to feel it.

She must expect and demand right conduct. She can do this by giving her pupils a reason for her demands. When she has made them see "the why," they—with her aid—will govern themselves.

Transgression of law means punishment. If pupils do wrong, they know that they need a punishment of some kind. If they are made to see their wrong, they won't resent the punishment.

The teacher should keep her promises. Of course she should not promise that which she can not do. But her word must be good. If she promises a treat, she should be sure to give it.

And also, if she promises a whipping, she should be sure to give it.

Fit the punishment to the offense. If the hands have done wrong, punish them. If the pupil has committed the sin, put the pupil in disgrace, etc.

Make, "keeping in" a novelty rather than a daily occurrence.

Use corporal punishment as a last resort. But if it is necessary, to do it: it may be "the makin' of the boy."

LESSON VII.

(Supervision of the Playgrounds.)

"All who joy would win must share it; Happiness was born a twin".

This does not mean—as it does in some places—to be a policeman.

Enter into the sport of the children. Try to be expert in the games. In other words, "be a hero."

When the teacher is near, everything will go smoothly. Disputes and quarrels will be reserved for home use. There will be a certain satisfied feeling, when work is resumed, in the anticipation of future pleasures.

LESSON VIII.

(Handling of Classes.)

"New occasions teach new duties."

This should be done in an orderly way. Commands for passing to and from recitation seats should be given.

If class is sent to the board, have a certain time to work and a certain time to erase, etc.

If there is no crayon rack, have one pupil pass the crayon around and then collect it.

LESSON IX.

(The Recitation Period.)

"Method is the hinge of business."

1. *Time—*
Primary classes—from ten to twenty minutes.
Intermediate classes—from ten to twenty minutes.
Grammar class—from ten to thirty minutes.

2. *Methods—*

The question method is probably about the best for primary classes.

The topic method can be used in primary classes for language work. Of course it is used in History, Geography, etc.

Concert work is good, if used once in a while. It is quite necessary to the life and interest in primary classes.

Some written work should be given every day. Children remember well the things they hear, see, and write.

3. *Assignment—*

A part of the recitation period should be used for the assignment of the next lesson. Talk to the pupils about the things that you want them to be sure to know. Point out the parts that you think will require the most study, etc. Tell them how to get it. This can be done with little people. Tell them how to study their reading lesson or their number work, or their spelling.

4. *Encouragement—*

If pupils do well, tell them so. If a poor pupil does fairly well, remark about it. If the work is poorly done, speak disappointedly about it, also remark that you expect something better the next time.

5. *Life—*

The children must be kept awake. Call on every pupil in the class. Be quick. Always be interested and your pupils will be interested.

Lesson X.

(The Study Period.)

"To read without reflection is like eating without digesting."

There must be a program of recitations and periods of study. The pupils must learn to do the same things at the same time each day. This teaches them system.

If the lesson has been properly assigned, and the time for study has already been fixed, half the problem has been solved.

This is a very important one. If the pupils are kept busy, the discipline is easy. And they must be kept busy.

It is a great thing to know how to study. Try to teach that.

While hearing a recitation, try to keep your eye on those who are studying. Impress upon their minds that they don't need watching; nevertheless watch them all the time.

Conclusion.

If the teacher is prepared to do her work, if the school grounds are made beautiful, if school hygiene is well attended to, if the entrance and dismissal of pupils is orderly, if the opening exercises are interesting to the children, if the teacher truly governs her pupils, if the classes are handled systematically, if the recitation is lively, and if the pupils are taught how and how much to study, the question of school management is absolutely settled.

Blackboard Reading Lessons

(Preparatory to Reading The Wide Awake Primer.)

Miss Elizabeth Willey and Miss Minnie L. Baker
Albuquerque Public Schools.

INTRODUCTION.

Several days, in fact, several weeks, should be spent at blackboard reading preparatory to the use of the text book. The vocabulary of the first forty or fifty pages of the primer should be taught in script at the blackboard before the children are asked to purchase their books The teacher should use the words in original sentences and stories, avoiding those used in the primer in order that the interest in the stories of the books may not be destroyed. When the text book is first used the change from script to print is made. The change will be readily made if the teacher will exercise care in not giving too much help.

The following ten lessons are suggestive of what the teacher may use for blackboard exercises. Note the large amount of drill; the many sentences and the small vocabulary.

J. E. C.

Sight words used in the ten lessons:

See the	John	This is
ball	I like	look
bird	little	look
dog	my	to play
Grace	doll	a boy
Kate	Ned	a girl
		good morning

First Day

(Sight Reading.)

See the (picture of a ball).
See the (picture of a book).
See the (picture of a cat).
See the (picture of a nest).
See the, (picture of birds).
See the (picture of a girl).
See the (picture of a mouse).
See the (picture of a top).
See the (picture of a hat).
See the (picture of a cap).
See the (picture of a box).
See the (picture of a fish).
See the (picture of a chair).
See the (picture of steps).

Second Day.

(Ball; bird; dog).
See the ball.
See the bird.
See the dog.
(Review first day sentences.)

Third Day.

(Grace; John)

Grace sees the ball.
Grace sees the bird.
Grace sees the dog.
John sees the ball.
John sees the dog.
John sees the.bird.
See the ball, John.
See the dog. Grace.
See the bird, John.
See the ball, Grace.
See the ball, John.
(Also use pictures of objects in sentences as on first day).

FOURTH DAY.

(I like; little).
I like Grace.
I like John.
I like the bird.
I like the ball.
I like the dog.
I like little Grace.
I like little John.
I like the little dog.
I like the little bird.
I like the little ball .
I see the little bird.
I see the little ball.
I like the little (picture of ball).
I like the little (picture of bird).
John likes the little dog.
Grace likes the little bird.
Grace sees the little ball.
John likes the little ball.

FIFTH DAY, REVIEW

I; like; the bird; the dog; the ball; John; Grace; see; little, sees; likes.
Read sentences of first four days.

SIXTH DAY.

(First Ten Minutes).

My; This is.

This is John.
This is Grace.
This is my little bird.
This is my little dog.
This is my little ball.
My ball is little.
My top is little.
My hat is little.
My dog is little.
My cat is little.

(Second ten minutes).

Grace likes my little bird.
John likes my little dog.
Grace sees my little ball.
John sees the ball.
I see the ball.
I like the ball.
This is my ball.
This is my little dog.
I like the little dog.
(Third ten minutes:—Review all the reading and erase.)

SEVENTH DAY.

(First ten minutes.

Grace is a girl.
John is a boy.
I like a girl.
I like a boy.
I see a little boy.
I see a little girl.
John likes a boy.
Grace likes a boy.
John likes a girl.
Grace likes a girl.

(Second ten minutes.)

John sees a little girl.
Grace sees a little boy.
See a boy.
See a girl.
See a ball.
I like a boy.
I like a little boy.
I see a little girl.
I see a little boy.
I see my dog.
I see my ball.
I see my bird.

EIGHTH DAY.

(First ten minutes)

Kate; Ned; Good-morning.

Good morning, Grace.
Good morning, John.
Grace is a little girl.
John is a boy.
Good morning, little boy.
Good morning, little girl.
Kate is a girl.
Kate is little.
Kate is a little girl.
This is Kate.
Good morning, Kate.

(Second ten minutes)

This is Ned.
Ned is a boy.
Ned is a little boy.
Ned likes my dog.
Good morning, Ned.
Good morning, Kate.
Kate is a little girl.
Ned is a little boy.
Grace is a little girl.
John sees Ned.
Grace sees Kate. ..

(Remaining time for review)

NINTH DAY.

(First ten minutes)

Look; to play; doll.

Look, Ned; Grace, look.
Look, look, look.
Look, Kate, see my bird.
Look Grace, see my ball.
Look, John, see my dog.
This is my doll.
Grace likes my doll.

Kate is my doll.
I like my doll.
This is my doll.
Good morning, little doll.

(Second ten minutes)

I like to play.
Grace likes to play.
Kate likes to play.
John likes to play.
Ned likes to play.
Look, look, see my doll.
Look, Ned see my ball.
Look, look, look.
Look, see the birds.
Look, Grace, look.
(Remaining time for review)

Tenth Day, Review

Look, look.
Look, Grace, look.
See the little birds.
See the little birds.
See the little birds, Grace.
See my doll.
See my little dog.
Look, look, see my doll.
See my doll, Grace.
This is my doll.
This is my little doll.
Kate is my doll.
Kate is my little doll.
This is Kate.
This is John.
This is Ned.
Good morning, John.
Good morning, Ned.
John is a little boy.
Ned is a little boy.
Grace is a little girl.

Physical Training

Rupert F. Asplund.

Lesson I.

The object—to develop the body and to make it able to do the will of the intellect. It involves recreation and rest. The need of physical training for rural New Mexican children.

Exercise 1.—

Body erect, heels together, feet at an angle of 60 degrees, chin high, eyes front, arms hanging at side—this is the position at the beginning of each exercise. Inhale easily and slowly, filling the chest. Then exhale slowly and easily. Repeat four times, increasing gradually from day to day to sixteen. In this and all following exercises, breathe deep, full breaths.

Lesson II.

Conditions: room well ventilated; temperature moderate; space for free movement; exercise, interesting; teacher enthusiastic.

Time: ten minutes regularly each day; at other times during the day when the children need rest from study.

Exercise 2.—

Swing right arm front and back of hip, eight movements, increasing to sixteen. Then left arm. Then alternately. Then simultaneously. With upper arms held at the sides, move right forearm up as far as possible and back to position eight times, increasing to sixteen. Then left fore-arm. Then alternately. Then simultaneously.

Lesson III.

Two periods of physical development, six to nine years of age and nine to fourteen. The exercises should be adapted to each. A study of physical defects necessary on the part of the teacher. The correlation of physical training and physiology.

Exercise 3.—

Turn head horizontally to the right four times, then to the left four times. Then alternate.

Bow head to the front four times, then to the right, then to the left, then back. Combine movements to front and back. Combine movements to right and left.

Lesson IV.

In the first period, the child needs such exercises as conform to natural activities and which tend to stimulate the circulation, respiration, and the nutritive functions. Large muscle groups only should be exercised. The play forms of gymnastics meet this requirement. Motion games. Marching.

Exercise 4.—

Stand erect with arms folded. Rise slowly on the toes as high as possible. Then lower heels slowly to the floor. Repeat eight times. Breathe deeply throughout the exercise.

Lesson V.

In the second period, the exercises of the first period should be continued. Quicker, more diversified and complicated movements should be added. These are furnished to a large degree in walking and running games.

Exercise 5.—

Stand in the usual position (see Exercise 1.) Hold arms at side with fingers closed. Open the fingers straight, then close them, eight times, increasing gradually to sixteen. Repeat with both arms horizontal in front, then with arms vertical above the head.

Lesson VI.

Correct habits in sitting, standing, walking. Form correct habits in running, jumping, and other exercise. Caution against too strenuous play.

Exercise 6.—

Stand erect. Place both hands closed on the chest. Extend right arm horizontally in front eight times. Then left. Then alternately. Then simultaneously. Extend arms in the same from the floor at the same time putting the right foot down on toe and sole. Then spring with the right foot, raising it and putting the left foot down. Reat four times, increasing to eight.

Lesson IX.

Kinds of gymnastic exercise; head exercises, to secure correct poise of the head and chest; arm exercises, to secure, development of chest, shoulder blades and arms; trunk exercises, to strenghten the spine and waist muscles; balance movements to strengthen the ankles, bringing the blood into the extremities; breathing exercises, to expand the chest and develop lung power and to improve the circulation.

Exercise 9.—

Bend the body to the front, horizontally, four times, holding the hands at the waist. Then bend the body to right four times manner horizontally to the right and left. Then vertically above the head. Then down at the sides.

Lesson VII.

Outdoor versus indoor gymnastics. The New Mexico climate and sunshine are favorable to open air exercise. The importance of the school yard. Supervision by the teacher on the play ground.

Exercise 7.—

In this exercise, short pieces of wood may be used instead of dumb bells.

Stand with feet eight inches apart with a dumb bell or other weight in each hand. Bend the body with arms extended. Let the weights touch the floor, then raise the body to the standing position. Repeat eight times, increasing gradually to sixteen.

Lesson VIII.

The games with and without supervision should be encouraged: Baseball; wolf and sheep; drop the handkerchief; ball games of all sorts. Different games for boys and girls. Rules of play always to be observed.

Exercise 8.—

Raise right knee until the right foot is a foot above the floor. Give a spring with the left foot, raising it swiftly a foot as far as possible, then to the left then back. Alternate and combine movements.

LESSON X.

Results: better standing and sitting position; correct walking; correct breathing; better circulation; freedom of joints and flexibility of muscles; greater nerve power; self-possession instead of self-consciousness; more intellectuality, including clearer thinking and greater concentration.

Exercise 10.—

Devise combinations made up from the preceding exercises. Give exercises involving sawing, hammering and chopping motions.

Elementary Agriculture

(Text Book Adopted—Agriculture for Beginners by Burkett, Stevens and Hill; Ginn & Company, Chicago, Ill.)

SUPERINTENDENT A. B. STROUP.

LESSON I.

Define Agriculture. Discuss its place in the economy of nature. What is the relation of Agriculture to Commerce? Manufacturing? Mining? Distinguish between the science of Agriculture and the practice of Agriculture. Show how they are related. Why should Agriculture be taught in our schools? Define Horticulture. In what way is it related to Agriculture? Name some men prominent in Agriculture and Horticulture and state specifically the thing for which they are best known. Discuss briefly the advances made in Agriculture and Horticulture in the past few years. Give illustration of this advance. What is the relation of machinery to Agriculture? Discuss fully.

LESSON II.

Define soil; subsoil. How are they related? What is the relation of the soil to life—both animal and plant? Discuss the origin of soil. What agencies are at work producing soil? Explain fully the ways in which they work and the natural laws that act. (Heat, cold, water, snow, ice, plants, animals). In every neighborhood these agencies are at work. Point out their action to your pupils. What has flowing water to do with soil making?

Define Humus. How is it put into the soil?

Discuss tillage and its relation to soil improvement. Why is tillage necessary? What are the implements used in tillage? What is the value of air in the soil?

Of what use is water to the soil? Explain fully. Water in the soil is found in three forms, free water, capillary water, and film water; explain each. About how much water will an acre

of grass give off to the air in a day? Whence does this moisture come? How does it get there?

LESSON III.

, The Campbell System of Farming is a system of scientific
tillage by which the moisture of the soil is used to its greatest
limit. Explain the principles upon which this system is based.
Is it profitable to use this system of farming in other than dry
regions? Why? What is the value of deep plowing? If water is
necessary to plant life, why is it often times necessary to drain
fields? There are nine reasons for draining. What kinds of,
soil need draining?

How may soil be improved? (Cultivate well, drain well, add
humus and plant food.) Why is manure or fertilizer necessary?
Name some of the substances that are needed in the soil and
give the common material in which each is found.

LESSON IV.

All plants are made up of root, stem and leaves; define
each of these terms and state the work each does for the plant
as a whole. Beginning with the root, explain fully how the
food is taken up by the root hairs, is carried through the stem,
and then is acted upon in the leaves. What is the relation of
plants to the soil? Of tillage to plants? If after tilling a crop
the leaves of the plants droop, what conclusion would you
draw? What makes them droop? Plants receive nourishment
from the soil and the air. Explain. Define and explain Capillary Attraction, Osmosis.

The Legumes. Clover, peas, vetches, alfalfa. etc., have little
knotty, wartlike growths on the roots called tubercles. Explain
the cause of these tubercles and the work they do. What element of food do they supply? Whence does it come? Farmers
oftentimes take earth from an old alfalfa field and haul it and
spread it over a new alfalfa field. Why? What is meant by rotation of crops? Of what value is it to the farm? Give a system of crop rotation and reasons for your arrangement. How
do plants feed from the air? What do they take from the air?
What does the plant do with starch and sugar? How are they
prepared in the plant? Explain the use of the sap circulation.
Does it correspond exactly to the circulation of the blood in
animals? Why do trees, that have been girdled, die?

LESSON V.

What is the use of the flowers on the plants? Do all plants have flowers? What is a flower?. Take one apart and study its parts. Note carefully the stamen and pistils, the stigma and anthers, the pollen, and the ovary. Study the office of each of the above parts. Discuss pollination and fertilization What is meant by cross-fertilization? How are the different varieties of the same kind of a plant developed? There are perhaps one hundred different kinds of wheat; how were they obtained? What part do insects play in this work of fertilization? Why should bees be kept in an orchard? Is pollination ever effected by hand? What is a seed? What is fruit? What is a hybrid? What is its value?

Discuss the propogation of plants by budding, seeding and cutting. What is the value of each? What is layering? Explain its value. Discuss seed selection and explain the value of proper selection of seed. Tell of the improvement that has been made in wheat and corn by proper selection of seed. •

What are weeds? How are weeds propagated? Observe the need of care in having seed free from weed seed. Name some plant that is a weed in some countries and a profitable plant in others. Discuss methods of ridding fields of weeds; the best time to do so.

LESSON VI.

Discuss grafting and study the conditions necessary to make a successful graft. Can a peach be grafted on an apple tree? What are the conditions that govern in this regard? What is the difference between budding and grafting? Explain fully how each is done.

Tell how you would go about to plant an orchard. Suppose that there was no nursery from which to buy trees, how would you grow them. Tell how they should be planted and give reasons. Why are trees pruned? Discuss fully. How and when should trees be pruned?

LESSON VII.

Plants have diseases the same as animals do. What causes disease? What is mold? How does it spread? Are all molds harmful? Why is fruit heated before being canned? Tell about yeast and bacteria. Name some diseases of man that are caused by bacteria.

How may plant diseases be prevented?

1. By destroying all diseased leaves, twigs, or fruit.

2. By killing spores on the seeds before planting and thus keep them from growing.

3. By spraying the leaves and foliage with a poison that will prevent the germination of the spores.

4. By selecting those varieties of plants that resist disease.

5. By coating the wounds made by prunning, with tar, paint, or some substance that will prevent the spores from entering.

6. The disease often remains in the soil and for this try rotation of crops, as the same disease does not attack all crops alike.

Discuss the foregoing fully.

Study carefully a few common diseases of plants. "Fire blight" of pear and apple, oat and wheat, smut, the rust on oat and wheat, potato scab, the peach curl, the cotton wilt, and the fruit mold.

Lesson VIII.

Insects are divided into two classes, beneficial and harmful Name some of each. Study for a few minutes a typical insect to become acquainted with his make up and the way he makes his living. Some important things to know: 1. How does the particular kind of insect take his food? You may be able then to successfully combat him. 2. What is his life history? Is he first, egg, then larva, then have wings? If so, learn length of time in each stage. You will then be able to fight him. By learning all about him you know at what stage of his life history to make the attack. Study this life history of a few of the common insect pests. (San Jose scale, coddling moth, plum curculio, Cakeworm, tent caterpillar, peach borer, from the orchard; and the cabbage worm, chinch bug, plant louse, squash bug, weevil, Hessian fly, potato beetle, and tobacco worm, from the garden and field.) This is a common list and remedies for most of them are easily found. In this connection be sure to emphasize the value of birds to the farmer.

LESSON IX.

Make a study of farm crops .The census reports will furnish information as to the comparative value of the crops grown. Upon what is success in growing a crop dependent? Make a study of the development of some of the staple crops, tracing their improvement and development from the time they were wild plants. Cotton, corn, wheat, oats, tobacco, grass.

Discuss the proper preparation of the soil, kind of soil, tillage, etc., that the different crops require. Of what value is machinery in the production of farm crops. Study the storing of the crop and the precautions necessary for its safety. Emphasize the economic side of farming. The market is an important factor to be considered by the farmer. Note that there are times to feed the grain and times to sell it. Note also the value of selling in carload lots. The farmer should be the best business man. Why?

LESSON X.

Domestic Animals; trace their development from the wild animal. Discuss the adaptability of the different breeds of common stock to the purpose for which they are raised. Which is it, environment or inherited tendencies, that predominate in producing the type?

Study the different types of the horse, cow, sheep, and barn yard fowl. Note in what they differ, one type from the other, as the purposes for which they were bred differ. Learn the names of the different parts of a horse, cow, etc. Study the comparison between the length of parts. Examine in this way a well proportioned horse and then examine some that are not so well proportioned; compare.

Look up statistics upon the value of farm stock. What is the average price of the different breeds of horses, cattle, sheep, hogs, chickens. What does it cost to raise an animal? Does it pay? What kind will produce the greatest profit Give reasons for the answer. Give statistics upon the number and value of eggs sold in the United States. The number of pounds of butter made. Does it pay to keep chickens on a farm? Give reasons.

Give some time to the care of the animals. Their shelter food, water.

Civics for New Mexico

The powers of the government of New Mexico are distributed among three departments, the legislative, the executive and the judicial.

The legislative power is vested in the governor and a legislative assembly, consisting of a council and a house of representatives. Sessions are held biennially, commencing on the third Monday in January, in each of the odd numbered years, and are limited by Congress to 60 days.

The Council consists of 12 members, one from each of the twelve council districts.

The House of Representatives consists of twenty-four members, one from each representative district.

Members of Assembly receive $4.00 per day and mileage. Speaker of House and President of Council receive $6.00 and mileage.

All laws passed by the legislative department of New Mexico must be submitted to the Congress of the U. S. for approval.

Executive Department.

Governor.—The executive power of the Territory is vested in a governor, appointed by the president of U. S. and confirmed by the Senate of the U. S. His term of office is for four years, unless sooner removed by the president. The Governor receives a salary of $6,500.00; $3,000.00 of which is paid by the Department of the Interior.

Secretary.—The Secretary of the Territory is appointed by the President of U. S. and must be confirmed by U. S. Senate. His term of office is for 4 years, unless sooner removed by the President. In the absence of the Governor from the territory, or in case of his death, removal, resignation or other inability, the Secretary performs the duties of the Governor. He must

record and preserve all laws passed by the legislative department of territory and transmit same to federal authorities. He
must make a record of all executive acts of the territorial governor. His salary is $1,800.00 and fees.

Other Executive Officers and Their Salaries.—The Governor appoints the following executive officers: Attorney General, $3,500.00; Treasurer, $2,400.00; Auditor of public accounts,
$3,000.00; Traveling Auditor and bank examiner, $3,000.00;
Commissioner of Public Lands, $3,000.00; Superintendent of
the Penitentiary, $2,400.00; Superintendent of Public Instruc-
tion, $3,000.00; Irrigation Engineer, $2,400.00; Adjutant
General $2,400.00; Game and Fish Warden, $1,800.00; Captain of Mounted Police, $2,000.00; Librarian, $900.00.

These officers must be confirmed by the Territorial Council.

JUDICIAL DEPARTMENT

The judicial department is vested in a supreme court, district courts, probate courts, and justices of the peace.

Supreme Court.—The Supreme Court consists of a Chief
justice and six Associate Justices, appointed by the President
of U. S. for a term of four years and all measures of court
must be confirmed by the U. S. Senate.

The Attorney General is an official of the judicial department and represents the Territory in all judicial proceedings,
and also acts as legal advisor to all territorial officers.

The Clerk of the Supreme Court keeps its records and is appointed by the court and holds his office indefinitely.

The territory is divided into seven judicial dstricts, and each
district court is presided over by one of the Judges of the Supreme Court.

District Attorney.—The District Attorney is an officer of
the judicial department and is appointed by the Governor, for a
term of two years.

Clerk of District Court.—Clerks of district courts are appointed by the judges of the court for an indefinite period.

Probate Judge.—In every county there is a probate judge
elected by the people for a term of two years.

Justice Court.—In every precinct there is a Justice of the
Peace elected for a term of two years.

COUNTIES.

There are twenty-six counties in the Territory, and each is governed by a board of three County Commissioners, elected by the people for a term of two years, and their legislative powers include creating precincts on petition of fifty citizens of the locality where the precinct is proposed to be erected.

Other county officers elected by the people of the several counties for terms of two years are as follows:

Sheriff, Treasurer and ex-Officio Collector, Probate Judge, Probate Clerk and ex-Officio Recorder, Assessor, Superintendent of Schools and County Suveyor.

Municipal Corporations.—Municipal Corporations are of two classes, those of a population of 2,000 and upwards, which are called cities, and those with a population of from 1,500 to 2,000 which are known as incorporated towns. Communities having population of 250 may incorporate as villages.

The corporation authority in cities is vested in a mayor and a board of aldermen, while in towns it is vested in a board consisting of a mayor, four trustees and a recorder.

SCHOOL SYSTEM

Territorial Board of Education, consists of nine members, the Governor, Superintendent of Public Instruction, and seven members to be appointed by the Governor from the heads of territorial educational institutions, the President of St. Michael's College, Santa Fe, and the superintendents of schools in the four cities of the Territory, ranking highest in population at the time the appointment is made, and two of the seven must not be in the active service of teaching.

The principal duties of Territorial Board of Education, is to adopt text books and grant teachers' licenses.

The governor is the chairman of the Territorial Board of Education and the Territorial Superintendent of Public Instruct is secretary.

The Territorial Superintendent of Public Instruction is the principal educational officer and is appointed by the Governor ior a term of two years and his appointment must be confirmed by the Council.

It is his duty to visit the various counties in the interest of education, hold teachers' institutes, prepare courses of study for the public schools and for county normal institutes and to keep a record of the proceedings of the Territorial Board of Education.

The County Superintendent of Public Instruction is the principal school officer of the county, and it is his duty to visit all the schools in his county *as many* times each year, as the Board of Education may direct, and apportion the general and county school funds among the several school districts in the county. To have general supervision of the work of district school officers, appoint same when vacancies occur, divide or organize districts under certain conditions and to endorse all orders for money to be paid out by district. To receive annually a report from each district, and to make an annual report to the Territorial Superintendent of Public Instruction on or before October 15th, of each year.

School Directors.—Each school district is governed by three directors, one elected each year.

It is the duty of the Board of Directors to have general care and custody of all school property, provide for school sites, pay teachers' wages, purchase supplies, fuel, etc., and to provide for paying interest on school bonds.

In cities the school interests are looked after by a Board of Education, consisting of two members from each ward elected for a term of two years, who organize and maintain a system of graded schools, and make levies to meet all expenses.

SCHOOL AGE.

All children between the ages of seven and fourteen, who are not in attendance at some private school or not under physical disability, or who do not live more than three miles from a public school, are required by school officers to attend the public school "during the entire time such school is in session in each scholastic year in their respective school communities."

TERRITORIAL OFFICERS.

Governor .... William J. Mills
Secretary .... Nathan Jaffa
Attorney General .. .. Frank W. Clancy
Auditor .... William G. Sargent

Treasurer .... Miguel A. Otero
Superintendent of Penitentiary .... Cleofes Romero
Superintendent of Public Instruction .... Jas. E. Clark
Asst. Superintendent of Public Instruction .. Acasio Gallegos
Librarian .... Lola C. Armijo
Commission Public Lands .... Robert P. Ervien
Traveling Auditor and Bank Examiner .... Chas. V. Safford
Game and Fish Warden .... Thos. P. Gable
Superintendent of Insurance .... Jacobo Chavez
Oil Inspector .... Malaquias Martinez
Engineer (Irrigation) .... Vernon L. Sullivan
Captain Mounted Police .... Fred Fornoff

JUDICIARY.

Chief Justice .... William H. Pope
Associate Justices .... John R. McFie
      "   "   .... Ira A. Abott
      "   "   .... Frank W. Parker
      ..   .. Alfred W. Cooley
                              .... Merritt C. Mechem
      "   .... Edmond C. Abbott
Clerk .... Jose D. Sena

EXECUTIVE OFFICERS OF NEW MEXICO

Hon. W. H. Andrews, Delegate to Congress .... Albuquerque
Hon. . W. March, Surveyor General .... Santa Fe
Hon. H. P. Bardshar, Col. Int. Rev. .... Santa Fe
Hon. D. J. Leahy, United States Attorney ..... Las Vegas
Hon. C. M. Foraker, U. S. Marshal .... Albuquerque

FEDERAL OFFICERS OF UNITED STATES.

President .... Hon. W H. Taft
Vice President .... Hon. J. S. Sherman

CABINET OFFICERS.

Secretary of State .... Hon. P. C. Knox
Secretary of Treasury .... Hon. Franklin McVeagh
Secretary of War .... Hon. J. M Dickinson
Postmaster General .... Hon. F. H Hitchcock
Secretary of Navy .... Hon. G. v. L. Meyer

Secretary of Interior .... Hon. R. A. Ballinger
Attorney General .... Hon. G. W. Wickersham
Secretary of Agriculture .... Hon. J. S. Wilson
Secretary of Commerce & Labor .... Hon. Chas. Nagel

NATIONAL JUDICIARY.

Chief Justice .... Hon. M. W. Fuller
Associate Justice .... Hon. John M. Harlan
   "   " .... Hon. E D. White
   "   " .... Hon. Joseph McKenna
   "   " .... Hon. O. W. Holmes
   "   " .... Hon. W. R. Day
          .... Hon. W. H. Moody
          .... Hon. Charles A. Hughes
   "   " .... Hon. C. L. Lurton

EDUCATIONAL INSTITUTIONS OF NEW MEXICO

University of New Mexico .... Albuquerque
College of Agriculture and Mechanic Arts ...... Las Cruces
New Mexico Normal School .... Silver City
New Mexico Spanish-American Normal School .... El Rito
New Mexico School of Mines .... Socorro
New Mexico Military Institute .... Roswell
Institute For Deaf and Dumb .... Santa Fe
Institute For Blind .... Alamogordo
Museum of New Mexico .... Santa Fe

OTHER TERRITORIAL INSTITUTIONS.

New Mexico Insane Asylum .... Las Vegas
New Mexico Penitentiary .... Santa Fe
New Mexico Reform School .... Springer
Miners' Hospital of New Mexico .... Raton

SCHOOL LANDS.

By the Organic Act establishing the Territory approved
Sept. 9th, 1850 and declared in force December 13, 1850, the
Federal Government granted sections 16 and 36 in each township to the schools of the territory. These sections cannot be
sold, but the income from leasing is considerable and such income is apportioned among the counties of the territory in pro-

portion to the number of children in each county. The county superintendent in turn apportions amount received by county among the districts according to number of children in the several districts. The number of acres included in this grant amounts to 4240080. The bill now before congress contemplates reserving sections 2 and 32 also for school purposes. ·

By the Act of Congress approved June 21, 1898, the following grants were made to the educational institutions:

	Acres.
University	111080
Agricultural College	100000
Normal Schools	100000
School of Mines	50000
Mililary Institute	50000
Reform School	50000
Blind Asylum	50000
Deaf and Dumb Asylum	50000

Some Important Provisions of the Statehood bill now Before the Senate of the United States

The qualified electors of New Mexico to choose delegates to frame the constitution.

Convention for the purpose of framing the constitution for the proposed state of New Mexico.

Within thirty days after the approval of the statehood act, the Governor of New Mexico shall order an election for choosing delegates to the convention; said election to be held not earlier than sixty days nor later than ninety days after approval of the act.

Delegates elected shall meet in the Hall of Representatives at Santa Fe at twelve o'clock on the fourth Monday after their election and shall remain in session not more than sixty days. After organization they shall declare on behalf of the people that they adopt the Constitution of the United States and may then proceed to frame the constitution which should be republican in form and make no disinction in civil or political rights on account of race or color and shall not be repugnant to the Constitution of the United States and the principles of the Declaration of Independence.

The state convention shall provide by ordinance irrevocable without the consent of the United States and the people of said state that there shall be toleration of religious sentiment, prohibition of polygamous or plural marriages, and the prohibition of sale, barter, or giving of intoxicating liquor to the Indians and that provision shall be made for the establishment and maintenance of a system of public schools; that the state shall never enact any law restricting or abridging the right of suffrage on account of race, color, or previous condition of servitude and that ability to read, write, speak, and understand the English language sufficiently well to conduct the duties of the office without the aid of an interpreter shall be a necessary qualification of all state officers and members of the state legislature.

That the capital of the state until changed by electors shall be at the city of Santa Fe; that no election shall be called for this purpose prior to the 31st day of December, 1925.

(There are other provisions which may not be changed without the consent of the United States aside from those mentioned.)

When the constitution has been made in accordance with principles laid down by the Senate bill, the convention shall provide for the submission of said constitution to the people of New Mexico for ratification at an election which shall be held on the date named by said convention not earlier than sixty days nor later than ninety days after said convention adjourns. If a majority of the legal votes cast at the election shall reject the constitution, the Governor of the Territory shall reassemble the convention at a date not later than twenty days after the date of receipt by the Governor of documents showing such rejection and a new constitution shall be framed and the same proceedings shall be taken in regard thereto as if the constitution were being oriignally prepared.

When the convention shall have been duly ratified and certified to the President of the United States and to Congress for approval and if Congress approves the constitution and the separate provisions thereof or if the President approves the same and Congress fails to disapprove same during the next regular session thereof, the President shall certify said facts to the Governor of New Mexico who shall, within thirty days after receipt of said notification from the President of the United States issue his proclamation for the election of the state and county officers. the members of the state legislature and representatives of Congress and all other officers provided for in said constitution. Said election to take place not earlier than sixty days nor later than ninety days after the proclamation by the Governor ordering same. If admitted under the proposed bill New Mexico will have 'two representatives in Congress elected at large. When the election of state and county officers, members of the legislature, and representatives to Congress, and other officers shall have been properly elected and their election certified, the Governor of the Territory of New Mexico shall certify the result of said election to the President of the United States who thereupon shall immediately issue his procla- mating announcing the result of said election and upon the is- suance of said proclamation of the President of the United States the proposed state of New Mexico shall be deemed ad- mitted by Congress into the Union by virtue of this act on equal footing with other states. Until the state is so admitted the county and territorial officers of said territory including the Delegate in Congress thereof elected at the general election of 1908 shall continue to discharge the duties of their respective offices in force in the territory, provided that no session of the territorial legislative assembly shall be held in 1910.

. The proposed bill provides for the granting of Sections 2, 16, 32, and 36 in every township for the support of the com- mon schools.

The bill provides for the following grants for educational in- stitutions: University, two hundred thousand acres; for schools and asylums for deaf, dumb and blind, one hundred thousand acres; normal schools, two hundred thousand; agricultural and mechanic arts college, one hundred fifty thousand acres. (The national appropriation heretofore annually paid for the Agri- cultural and Mechanical College to said territory, shall, until further order of Congress continue to be paid to said state for the use of said institution) ; the School of Mines, one hun- dred fifty thousand acres; Military Institutes, one hundred thousand.

Schools, colleges, and universities thus provided for shall remain under the exclusive control of said state and no part of the proceeds arising from the sale or disposal of any lands granted herein for educational purposes shall be used for the support of sectarian or denominational schools, colleges, or uni- versities.

Five per cent of the proceeds of sales of public lands lying within said state which shall be sold by the United States, after deducting all expenses of such sales, shall be paid to said state to be used as permanent inviolable fund, the interest of which only shall be expended for the support of the common schools in said state.

Lands east of the line between ranges 18 and 19, east of the New Mexico principal meridian shall not be sold for less than five dollars per acre. The lands west of said line shall not be sold for less than three dollars per acre.

The state when admitted shall constitute one judicial district and the said district shall for judicial purposes, be attached to the eighth judicial district.

Members of the legislature elected at the election may assemble at Santa Fe, organize. and elect two Senators of the United States in the manner now prescribed by the constitution and the laws of the United States.

The sum of one hundred thousand dollars or so much thereof as may be necessary is appropriated from the United States treasury to defray all and every kind and character of expense incident to the elections and convention provided for in the bill.